Paraeducators in Schools

Paraeducators in Schools

Strengthening the Educational Team

Anna Lou Pickett
Kent Gerlach
Robert Morgan
Marilyn Likins
Teri Wallace

pro·ed
An International Publisher

8700 Shoal Creek Boulevard
Austin, Texas 78757-6897
800/897-3202   Fax 800/397-7633
www.proedinc.com

© 2007 by PRO-ED, Inc.
8700 Shoal Creek Boulevard
Austin, Texas 78757-6897
800/897-3202   Fax 800/397-7633
www.proedinc.com

Library of Congress Cataloging-in-Publication Data

Paraeducators in schools : strengthening the educational team / Anna Lou Pickett ... [et al.].
    p. cm.
  ISBN-13: 978-1-4164-0217-6
  ISBN-10: 1-4164-0217-9
  1. Teachers' assistants—Training of—United States. 2. Teaching teams—United States.   I. Pickett, Anna Lou.
  LB1734.5.P37 2007
  371.14'124—dc22

                                                                    2006012505

Art Director: Jason Crosier
Designer: Nancy McKinney
This book is designed in Fairfield LH, Gill Sans, and Italia.

Printed in the United States of America

  2 3 4 5 6 7 8 9 10   10 09 08 07

Dedicated to the many paraeducators who inspired us.

Contents

3   Exploring the Roles of the Paraeducator in Instruction   55

Robert Morgan

**4   Promoting Positive Behavior:
    What Works and What Doesn't   75**

Marilyn Likins and Debra Andrews

Foreword

School systems and education practices nationwide are undergoing many changes, and one of the more significant changes is the ongoing evolution in the roles of paraeducators. *Paraeducators in Schools: Strengthening the Educational Team* is a highly readable, research-based, relevant training resource for personnel developers in community colleges, postsecondary technical schools, adult-education providers, and in-service training programs provided by local school districts. In addition to identifying the roles and responsibilities of paraeducators and the importance of teamwork and communication, the text offers paraeducators practical information to use for their work in instruction, behavior intervention, and problem solving. The case studies in each chapter enliven the book and provide real-life situations to help paraeducators relate the information to their day-to-day work. The discussion questions and activities serve as extensions to the material and will help foster dialogues among administrators, teachers, paraeducators, and personnel developers about how the information applies to the needs of their schools and communities.

The text addresses essential issues and standards for the preparation of community college students. This valuable text also provides community college faculty members with resources they can build on to prepare students for careers in education and other areas in the human services field. Community college students who are interested in entering the education workforce are caring, concerned individuals who use life experiences and commitment to help others. Paraeducators require more than love and patience, however; they need knowledge and skills that enable them to assist licensed practitioners in the delivery of education and other direct services for learners and their parents. The text contains curriculum content and teaching tools that faculty members can use to support their students' dedication and desire to learn and to become confident members of instructional teams. Additional applications for other areas of preemployment preparation can be used to train prospective paraeducators through venues such as career–technical schools, adult-education programs, and vocational programs operated by school systems and related provider agencies.

This book is an excellent resource not only for preemployment training but also for in-service preparation programs. The chapters address daily concerns faced by paraeducators, teachers, administrators, and others with whom they work. The book is a practical and effective tool for creating in-service and career development programs for paraeducators. The user-friendliness of the content, activities, and layout increases the likelihood that district administrators, principals, and staff developers will gain a better understanding of what they need to know and be able to do to ensure that paraeducators are highly skilled and appropriately supervised. The overall book—or single chapters—can provide a framework for creating opportunities for paraeducators' career development or for strengthening teacher and paraeducator teams. For example, individual teacher and paraeducator teams can use the book as a resource for improving their team's performance through district-approved independent study, or paraeducator study groups can use chapter discussion questions and activities within and across schools by meeting or by using online activities.

We thank the authors for providing our field with this invaluable resource for increasing the knowledge and skills of its primary audience: paraeducators, as well as the teachers and administrators with whom they work. In so doing, this text can be a catalyst for ensuring that local policy and practice reflect research-based findings that lead to high learner outcomes for all students.

Peggy Hayden and *Susan Simon*

Peggy Hayden is the coordinator of paraeducator policy and professional development initiatives for the Rhode Island Department of Education. Her work is carried out through the Technical Assistant Program, located at Rhode Island College. She facilitated the work of the national taskforce that produced the document *Strengthening and Supporting Teacher and Paraeducator Teams: Guidelines for Paraeducator Roles, Supervision, and Preparation.*

Susan Simon is a professor at Kirkwood Community College, located in Cedar Rapids, Iowa. She has established systems and developed curriculum for both pre- and in-service training programs to increase the availability of a highly qualified paraeducator workforce. As a consultant to the Iowa Department of Education, she contributed to the development of the statewide paraeducator certification system.

Preface

The roles and responsibilities of paraeducators nationwide have changed dramatically since they were introduced into general, special, multilingual, Title I, and other compensatory education programs. In today's schools, under the direction of teachers, paraeducators provide instructional and support services for learners who can benefit from individualized (differentiated) education programs and personalized attention. Provisions in the No Child Left Behind Act of 2001 and the reauthorization of the Individuals with Disabilities Education Act of 1997 and 2004 recognize the evolution in the roles and responsibilities of paraeducators and now require all educators, including paraeducators, to be highly qualified.

Paraeducator, paraprofessional, teacher's aide, instructional assistant, educational assistant, transition trainer, job coach, therapy assistant, and home visitor are just a few of the titles assigned to staff who, while working under the direction of a teacher or another professional practitioner, assist with the delivery of instructional and other direct services. This text is designed to serve as a resource for community college instructors and staff development personnel who prepare paraeducators to work in early childhood, elementary, middle, and secondary school programs.

Chapter 1 contains (a) an overview of why paraeducators have become key members of education teams, (b) a discussion of the distinctions between teacher and paraeducator roles, and (c) a discussion of the roles of principals and other administrators in ensuring that paraeducators are appropriately supervised and prepared. Chapters 2 through 5 address in greater depth the roles and responsibilities of paraeducators and their training needs in the following areas: (a) skills all paraeducators need to be effective team members; (b) behavior intervention and management skills and knowledge required by paraeducators; (c) instructional strategies that support learners and learning; (d) communication and problem-solving strategies that strengthen paraeducator contributions to team performance; and (e) opportunities for career development.

The text is based on a philosophy that recognizes the value of a highly skilled paraeducator workforce that assists teachers in providing quality education for all learners. The goals and activities incorporate currently recognized best practices in adult education. The format in each of the chapters follows a similar pattern that includes instructional objectives, definitions of key terms, competency-based instructional content, discussion questions, case studies, and other learning activities.

The overall training goals for the text are to provide paraeducators with skills and knowledge that will enable them to

1. demonstrate an awareness of federal laws, state policies, and local regulations that influence paraeducator employment, roles and responsibilities, preparation, and supervision;

2. describe the roles of district administrators, program directors, and principals in developing standards, systems, and personnel practices that strengthen and support the work of teacher and paraeducator teams;

3. describe the roles of principals in the management of paraeducators;

4. describe the roles of teachers as leaders of instructional teams and supervisors of paraeducators;

5. describe those teacher responsibilities that must not be delegated to paraeducators and those that may be shared;

6. describe the roles of paraeducators as team members who assist in the delivery of education and related services to learners or their families;

7. demonstrate an ability to follow lesson plans, Individualized Education Programs, and behavior intervention plans developed by teachers;

8. demonstrate an ability to use differentiated instructional strategies developed by teachers to meet the needs of individual learners;

9. practice ethical standards of conduct that respect diversity and the human and legal rights of learners, families, and coworkers; and

10. demonstrate an ability to communicate and share information effectively with teachers, learners and their families, administrators, and other school personnel.

Acknowledgments

We would like to thank the many colleagues who supported and assisted with the preparation and review of this text. Their contributions provided us with current best practices associated with the employment, training, role clarification, and supervision of paraeducators. A very special thanks to Mary Ellen Heiner for her editorial assistance and to Debra Andrews for her contibutions to Chapter 4.

The staff at PRO-ED has given us unfailing encouragement, guidance, and advice. We especially appreciate the support of Beth Rowan, Sue Carter, Chris Anne Worsham, Kathy Synatschk, Matt Synatschk, Joshua Jeffrey, Jason Crosier, and Nancy McKinney.

We also want to recognize the thousands of dedicated paraeducators and their supervisors who encouraged us to write this text. Their support is greatly appreciated.

Paraeducators: Their Roles and Responsibilities

1

Anna Lou Pickett

Throughout the 20th century, significant changes occurred in the delivery and availability of education services in school districts across the United States. In less than 100 years, the majority of the U.S. population moved from family farms and small towns to large urban centers, and from there into suburbs. New education systems emerged as small schools gave way to large, consolidated districts. Increasing numbers of new immigrants helped create a multiethnic, multicultural, and multilingual society. Advances in medical science enabled more children with disabilities and life-threatening health-care needs to live and to thrive. The movement into the age of computers and other technologies created new career opportunities and challenged educators to find more effective ways to prepare a workforce requiring new, more complex skills. An expanding economy led to higher standards of living for many families and improved education for their children while, at the same time, the numbers of children and youth who lived in poverty and who came from educationally disadvantaged backgrounds increased.

This chapter provides a foundation for those chapters that follow. It opens with a series of case studies that describe the roles paraeducators play in general, multilingual, Title I, and special education programs. It continues with an overview of the issues and events that caused policy makers to rely on paraeducators to support the program and administrative functions of teachers. It moves on to a discussion of (a) distinctions in teachers' and paraeducators' roles in the delivery of instructional and related services; (b) responsibilities of paraeducators in the delivery of education and other direct services to learners and their parents; (c) a model code of ethics for paraeducators; and (d) the differences in the roles of district administrators, principals, and teachers in ensuring that paraeducators are well prepared and appropriately supervised. Definitions of key terms used in the chapter are provided, along with discussion questions and suggested activities to enhance paraeducators' learning.

Learning Objectives

After studying the information in this chapter and participating in class discussions and other activities, paraeducators will

1. define the term *paraeducator;*
2. describe how court-ordered mandates, legislative actions, and other historical events caused Local Education Agencies (LEAs) to turn to paraeducators to assist teachers;
3. discuss reasons for increased reliance on paraeducators, with greater emphasis placed on their instructional and learner support roles in today's schools;
4. describe the distinctions between the roles and responsibilities of teachers and paraeducators in the instructional process and the delivery of other direct services to learners and their families;
5. describe provisions in recent federal legislation concerned with enhancing the performance of teacher and paraeducator teams;
6. describe the responsibilities of administrators in State Education Agencies (SEAs) and LEAs in developing standards and systems to ensure that paraeducators are effectively trained and appropriately supervised to carry out their assigned tasks; and
7. describe the differences in the management and supervisory roles of principals and teachers in assessing the overall performance of paraeducators and monitoring the day-to-day work of paraeducators.

Key Terms and Definitions

The following key terms and definitions will be used throughout this chapter.

Competencies. Specific skills and knowledge required to perform their job by paraeducators who are assigned to different programs or positions.

Credentialing. Systems designed to certify that paraeducators have mastered the knowledge and skills required for entry to or higher levels of paraeducator positions. Most states do not have a credentialing system for paraeducators. States that have created credentials may call them a "permit," "license," or "certificate."

Family. Parents or others who have responsibility for a child's care and well being.

Institutions of Higher Education (IHEs). Two-year colleges that offer associate of arts or associate of science degrees and 4-year colleges or universities that offer bachelor of arts, master's, and doctoral programs.

Learner. School-age students and young children. Because this text may be used to train paraeducators who work in early childhood programs or elementary, middle, and secondary schools, the terms *learners, children, youth,* and *students* are used interchangeably.

Local Education Agency (LEA). A local or intermediate school district that has responsibility for providing education and related services to learners and their families.

Paraeducator. Paraprofessional, instructional assistant, teacher's aide, education technician, occupational and physical therapy assistant or aide, speech–language pathology assistant, transition trainer, job coach, health-care aide, and home visitor are just a few of the titles used in school districts nationwide for support personnel who (a) are supervised by teachers or other licensed professionals, and (b) assist with the delivery of instructional and related services for learners and their families (adapted from Pickett, 1989). To reduce wordiness, the term *paraeducator* is used throughout this text. There are times, however, when, to maintain historical accuracy or to refer to a specific discipline, it is more appropriate to use other titles. For example, in the sections that describe the reasons this new category of support personnel were introduced into public schools, the terms *teacher's aide* and *paraprofessional* are used.

Skill standards. Statements that describe job functions or tasks related to competency areas established for an occupation or profession. Standards include skills, knowledge, and performance indicators to ensure that individuals have mastered required skills. The skills may be learned on the job or during preservice training.

Stakeholders. Agencies and organizations with responsibility for or concerns about improving the quality of education and related services for learners with different needs. They may include state and local education agencies; IHEs; unions; organizations representing different professional disciplines (e.g., teachers, therapists, administrators); and advocacy groups concerned with protecting the human and civil rights of learners and their families.

State Education Agency (SEA). Department of Education, Department of Public Instruction, or another agency that is responsible for establishing and administering statewide policies, guidelines, or regulations to ensure the quality of education for all learners in early childhood, elementary, middle, and secondary school programs.

Supervisor. Teachers and other professional practitioners who are responsible for integrating paraeducators into the instructional team. Teachers' supervisory responsibilities include planning, scheduling and assigning tasks for paraeducators based on their experience and training, directing and monitoring the day-to-day work of paraeducators, providing feedback about paraeducator performance, developing and conducting on-the-job coaching based on identified training needs, and sharing relevant information with principals about paraeducator strengths and training needs. Although there may be other professional practitioners who have supervisory responsibility for support personnel (i.e., occupational and physical therapists, speech–language pathologists, librarians, nurses, early childhood specialists), the term *teacher* is used throughout the text unless the reference is to a specific discipline or occupation.

Setting the Stage

The following and similar scenarios play out daily in schools across the country. They reflect paraeducators' increased participation in the delivery of instructional and related services for children and youth who have a wide range of learning and language-related needs. They also indicate the need for SEAs and LEAs to form partnerships with IHEs, professional organizations that represent different education disciplines, unions, and other stakeholders that (a) define differences in the roles of teachers and paraeducators in the delivery of instructional and related services; (b) establish policies and personnel practices to improve the contributions paraeducators make to the delivery of education and related services; (c) provide opportunities for standardized, systematic training and career development for paraeducators; and (d) prepare teachers for their emerging roles as supervisors of paraeducators.

 JIM

Jim, a paraeducator with 4 years' experience in a middle school special education resource room, has had very little formal training. The on-the-job training provided by teachers and other work-related experiences have taught him a great deal; moreover, he has always received good evaluations from the principal. This year, Jim has a new assignment. He is supporting Peter, who has been diagnosed as having a severe learning disability in four general education classes: math, social studies, language arts, and health science. Peter also has physical disabilities that sometimes cause him to need assistance. Peter's Individualized Education Program (IEP) identifies the following responsibilities for the paraeducator assigned to work with him: (a) Tutor him using instructional interventions developed by the teachers to meet his identified learning needs, and (b) support him in the classroom and in other learning environments when physical assistance is required. The teachers in each of the four classes use different approaches and methods when working with Peter, and Jim is worried that his learning goals are not being met. Jim is particularly concerned that the teachers have different expectations about what his role in "their classroom" should be. On several occasions, two of the teachers asked Jim to assist other students with their lessons. Three of the teachers asked Jim to photocopy worksheets and grade papers for the entire class, and one of the teachers asked Jim to help arrange a field trip and then to make sure that all students returned their permission slips. Jim is not sure that the teachers should ask him to carry out these activities because Peter's IEP does not mention working with other students or assisting with other activities. Jim does not know who he should turn to find answers to his concerns.

SHARON

Sharon, a new paraeducator, was hired 2 days before the school year began and was assigned to a Title I program. She had attended a local community college and earned an AA degree in liberal arts. She was hired by the district's personnel director because her qualifications met the education requirements for paraeducators. She is responsible for tutoring several elementary school learners who can benefit from personalized attention.

Sharon met with Gloria, a teacher and coordinator of Title I classrooms, for an hour the first day of school. Gloria reviewed the purpose of Title I and the goals of the reading and math programs that Sharon would reinforce with the individual students she would work with. Since then, Gloria has developed weekly lesson plans for Sharon to follow and leaves the plans in Sharon's mailbox. Sharon and Gloria have different schedules and rarely see each other. If Sharon has questions about the plans and suggested activities, she asks other, more experienced paraeducators for ideas she might use to keep the students interested and to reinforce their learning goals. She also brings in books and games that her own children enjoy. Although Sharon does not always follow Gloria's lesson plans, she feels she is doing a good job because the students seem to enjoy the activities she plans for them.

MARILYN

Marilyn, a speech–language pathologist, is working with a therapy assistant for the first time in 10 years. She is pleased that Lhia, who is fluent in two Cambodian dialects, has been added to the team because many of the students in her caseload come from homes where one of the dialects is the primary language. Marilyn is concerned, however, because she has noticed that many parents seem to feel more comfortable speaking with Lhia about their children than with her. Marilyn feels strongly that it is her responsibility to share information with the children's parents about the strategies she is using to improve their speech. Although she and Lhia work well together, Marilyn is afraid that she will offend Lhia if she tells her to communicate with parents only after the two of them have discussed the information that should be shared with the parents.

CAMILLA

Camilla has worked as a paraeducator for 22 years. She started her career as a playground and lunchroom monitor. For the last 18 years, depending on the district's personnel needs, she has worked as an instructional assistant in Title I or special education programs. Camilla has learned a great deal about how to work with children and youth who have different learning needs by observing the teachers she has assisted over the years. She always looks forward to attending workshops for paraeducators when the district offers them, although they are only sporadically available. She is respected and well liked by teachers, administrators, students, and parents, and last year she was named "Paraeducator of the Year" at a statewide conference. This year Camilla has been assigned to work in an inclusive third-grade class with Rosalie, a first-year teacher. Although Rosalie is confident that she has the skills she needs to plan for and to teach the students, she is not sure about her ability to work with Camilla. She has had no training that prepared her to plan for and direct the day-to-day work of another adult, let alone someone who is old enough to be her mother and who has more than 20 years' experience. Things are not going well between them. Camilla has always seen herself as a team player; now she feels unappreciated and is becoming increasingly unhappy. She feels the tasks Rosalie asks her to perform do not exploit the skills she has worked so hard to acquire over the last 20 years. On the other hand, Rosalie finds Camilla to be slightly intimidating. She also believes that Camilla talks about her with other staff members because several teachers have made a point of telling her about how lucky she is to be working with Camilla.

Paraeducators in Education:
A Brief History of Their Employment

Whether you are an experienced or a beginning paraeducator, you may find yourself asking, "Why do I have to study history when all I want is to improve the skills I need to work with learners?" Many complex, inter-related reasons caused policy makers to turn to teacher's aides to provide support for the programs and administrative roles of teachers. The cur-rent roles of, responsibilities of, and relationships between teachers and paraeducators began with changes in education practices and systems that began more than 50 years ago and continue to the present. Pickett, Likins, and Wallace (2003) reported that the most significant factors that led to the employment of teacher's aides included the following:

1. Court-ordered mandates that require policy makers and adminis-trators to ensure all children and youth receive a free, public edu-cation of the highest quality in inclusive (integrated) schools
2. Provisions in federal laws that created programs to meet the needs of learners who live in poverty and come from education-ally disadvantaged family backgrounds
3. Increasing enrollment of learners from diverse cultural and lin-gual heritages
4. Increasing shortages of teachers in special education, multilin-gual education, and many academic program areas nationwide
5. Changes in traditionally recognized teacher roles

The 1950s

Interest in employing teacher's aides began in the mid-1950s and was fu-eled by (a) shortages of licensed teachers created by the "baby-boom" that occurred after World War II, and (b) the efforts of parents of children and adults with disabilities to gain access to education and other services in their local communities. During this period, two research projects were undertaken to test the appropriateness of employing teacher's aides to support teachers in the delivery of educational services.

The first project, sponsored by the Ford Foundation, took place in the Bay City, Michigan, schools. College-educated women who were not li-censed teachers were recruited and trained to perform noninstructional tasks that would allow teachers more time to plan and carry out lessons. The new employees provided clerical assistance; monitored playgrounds, lunchrooms, and study halls; duplicated instructional materials; helped maintain learning centers; and performed other routine classroom tasks. The idea of employing teacher's aides was not automatically accepted. Critics were concerned that teachers would be replaced with unqualified "cheap labor." By the time the Bay City project ended, however, policy makers and administrators were somewhat optimistic about the benefits of teacher's aides: To a limited extent, other districts in Michigan and a few other states began to hire teacher's aides to help reduce the impact of the teacher shortages (Ford Foundation, 1961).

The purpose of the second project, carried out at about the same time at Syracuse University, was to evaluate the effectiveness of teacher's aides in the special education programs that were slowly gaining a foothold across the country, in parent-sponsored programs and, to a lesser degree, in public schools (Cruickshank & Haring, 1957). Although the results of the Syracuse project, like the Bay City project, showed positive results, it would be more than 10 years before the benefits of employing paraprofessionals or teacher's aides to work alongside teachers and to assist them in both general and special education would be more fully tested (Gartner, 1971; Kaplan, 1977).

During this period, civil rights organizations began to challenge long-standing state and local laws, social customs, and education practices that (a) supported the education of African American students in "separate but equal" schools, and (b) denied children and youth with disabilities access to a publicly supported education.

The first of many events that took place over the next 30 years was a lawsuit filed by parents of African American children and youth and other advocates that asked the Supreme Court of the United States to end segregation in public schools. The suit was brought against the Topeka, Kansas, schools (*Brown v. Board of Education,* 1954). In their unanimous decision, the members of the United States Supreme Court ruled that (a) the social customs and state and local laws that approved of serving African American children and youth in "separate but equal schools" were inherently unequal, and (b) legally sanctioned racial segregation in public schools was unconstitutional. The Supreme Court decision did not automatically end racial segregation in U.S. schools—that would await passage of federal and state laws and advocates' ongoing efforts for upholding the rights of learners and their families to change social customs and attitudes.

The 1960s

During the 1960s, the Civil Rights Movement entered a new, more active phase. Dr. Martin Luther King, Jr., and other advocates for change became aware that if the goals of *Brown v. Board of Education* were to be achieved, segregation would need to end in housing, higher education, and a wide range of public and private sector service-delivery systems. Coalitions of educators and other human services providers; college students; religious leaders; and advocates for children and adults who lived in poverty, women, and seniors citizens participated in nonviolent protests that helped focus the nation's attention on social, education, economic, and political inequities. Separately and together, advocates for the different groups pressured public officials to create programs and policies that would improve the quality of life for all Americans. Their goals included removing barriers to quality education for all learners, improving and providing access to better health care for children and adults, opening the doors to higher education, and increasing opportunities for career development and advancement for people from racial, cultural, and language minorities and for those who had disabilities. Their efforts led to the passage of laws that created Medicare and Medicaid, established Head Start, initiated Community Action Programs that would help restore neglected neighborhoods, and provided workforce development training for youth and adults who were unemployed or unprepared for existing jobs.

The results of many of the laws enacted during this period had a profound impact on our nation's schools. Among the most significant were several programs contained in the Elementary and Secondary Education Act (ESEA; 1965), including Title I, which was created to more effectively serve educationally and economically disadvantaged school-age children and youth. Other ESEA programs were established to meet the learning needs of increasing numbers of English language learners, Native Americans, and other students with different learning and language needs.

The 1970s and 1980s

In the 1970s, parents and their supporters, concerned that the rights of children and adults with disabilities were being overlooked, became more organized. Their goals included (a) closing large institutions that were little more than "warehouses" for people with mental retardation, mental illness, and other disabilities, and (b) establishing services that would enable their children to attend school and work and to live in their community.

Brown v. Board of Education served as a model for two successful lawsuits filed in federal district courts that challenged the right of states and local school systems to exclude learners with disabilities from public schools (*Mills v. Board of Education of the District of Columbia*, 1972; *Pennsylvania Association for Retarded Children v. the Commonwealth of Pennsylvania*, 1972). The decisions in both cases recognized the right of school-age students, regardless of the severity or nature of their disability, to a free, appropriate public education (FAPE).

Although the decisions in the two suits did not apply to other states, the victories in the federal courts encouraged families and other advocates across the country that represented children and adults with disabilities to become more assertive. The families and advocates reached out to members of the United States Congress; their efforts paid off with the passage of two major federal laws that required schools nationwide to provide special education and related services for all learners with disabilities: the Rehabilitation Act of 1973 and the Education for All Handicapped Children Act of 1975.

The Rehabilitation Act of 1973 (also known as the civil rights act for people with disabilities) addressed several related issues including (a) breaking down barriers nationwide that prevented children, youth, and adults from participating in elementary, secondary, and higher education; (b) health care; (c) career development programs; and (d) access to public buildings. Of particular importance to schools were two provisions contained in Section 504 of the Act that (a) guaranteed that no learner could be excluded from any public school activities on the basis of disabilities that include mental or physical impairment(s) that substantially limit one or more major life activity, and (b) added children and youth who have health and related conditions that may place them at risk (e.g., tuberculosis, AIDS, asthma, hepatitis, severe and chronic allergies, hyperactivity, attention-deficit disorder) to the definition of learners who must be served in general education classes.

The Education for all Handicapped Children Act of 1975 was retitled as the Individuals with Disabilities Education Act (IDEA; 1990). This federal legislation requires state and local education agencies to provide a free, appropriate public education in the least restrictive environment (LRE) for all school-age children and youth with disabilities without regard to the nature or severity of their disability. It also broke new ground by requiring LEAs to provide services for learners with disabilities based on IEPs developed cooperatively by parents, educators, and related service providers. Over the years, IDEA has been amended to require schools or other agencies to provide education for preschool-age children and transition services for teenagers. Other laws encouraged the development of programs to serve infants and toddlers (ages birth to 2 years) with disabilities and their families. The services provided by these programs are based on (a) individualized family service plans (IFSPs) for parents and young children, and (b) individualized transition plans (ITPs) for teenagers to prepare them to move from school to the world of work or higher education and to live independently or with support in the community. In the 1990s, IDEA expanded the definition of LRE by placing a priority on serving learners with disabilities in inclusive general education classes. Other important provisions in IDEA protect the rights to privacy and due process for learners and their families and provide guidelines for disciplinary procedures.

At the heart of the various laws enacted during the 1960s and 1970s was the recognition of the value of learner-centered education programs to meet the needs of children and youth with different instructional and language-related needs. Thus, to provide teachers with the support they needed to plan and carry out IEPs for learners with disabilities and to provide personalized attention for children and youth with other education needs, paraprofessional employment grew, and greater emphasis was placed on paraprofessionals' instructional and learner support roles. Increasingly their duties were expanded to include (a) providing one-to-one and small-group instruction; (b) carrying out behavior management and disciplinary plans developed by teachers; and (c) conducting outreach and support services for parents (Pickett, 1989).

Despite increased reliance on paraprofessionals throughout this period, SEAs and LEAs paid scant attention to the interrelated issues surrounding the roles, preparation, and supervision of paraprofessionals. Moreover, with rare exceptions, administrators and personnel developers in SEAs, LEAs, and IHEs did not join forces to address the emerging need of preparing teachers to effectively include paraprofessionals in instructional teams.

In fact, by the late 1980s, only 11 states had certification or regulatory systems that included standards for the roles, preparation, and supervision of paraprofessionals. The remaining states chose to develop nonbinding administrative guidelines that usually placed the responsibility for paraprofessional training on LEAs (Pickett, 1989). As a result, (a) distinctions in teacher and paraprofessional responsibilities were not always clearly defined; (b) similarities and differences in the knowledge and skills required by paraprofessionals working in different programs were not established; (c) teachers' roles in directing and monitoring the day-to-day work of paraeducators were not identified; and (d) training for paraprofessionals, when it did exist, was not based on statewide training standards or systems of personnel development linked to opportunities for advancement based on an individual's career preference.

Paraeducators in Education: The Present

In Greek, the meaning of *para* is "alongside of." With the advent of Title I in the 1960s and the introduction of special education programs in the 1970s, some LEAs began to use the title "paraprofessional" rather than teacher's aide to recognize personnel who worked alongside of teachers and assisted with the delivery of education and related services for learners and their parents. In today's schools, the roles of these newest members of instructional teams are continuing to change. Increasingly "they are becoming technicians who work alongside and assist teachers in all phases of the instructional process. As a result they are more appropriately described as *paraeducators*, just as their counterparts in law and medicine are designated as paralegals and paramedics" (Pickett, 1989, p. 1).

Despite the increased reliance on paraeducators, with greater emphasis on their learner support roles, by the mid-1990s the majority of SEAs and LEAs still had not begun to develop policies and personnel practices to ensure that paraeducators were prepared to carry out their assigned tasks as members of instructional teams. In 1997, amendments to IDEA required SEAs to establish standards and systems to ensure that a highly skilled paraeducator workforce was available to support teachers' program and administrative responsibilities. Provisions in the newly reauthorized IDEA 2004 are similar to those enacted in 1997. They (a) allow paraprofessionals who are appropriately trained and supervised—in accordance with state law, regulations, or written policy—to assist with the delivery of special education and related services to children and youth with disabilities, and (b) require SEAs to ensure that *all* education personnel have the skills and knowledge necessary to meet the identified needs of learners with disabilities.

In 2001, the Elementary and Secondary Education Act was given a new title—the No Child Left Behind Act (NCLB). Amendments to NCLB concerned with tapping the resources of the paraeducator are more specific than those in IDEA. NCLB Section 1119 (pp. 128–133) requires that SEAs or LEAs define paraeducator responsibilities, establish standards for their employment, and develop career development systems to ensure that all teachers and paraeducators are "highly qualified." (In addition, NCLB is the first federal law to specify that paraeducators are to be directed by qualified teachers.) The amendments require the following:

1. The standards must establish education and experiential requirements for paraeducators. All new paraeducators employed after January 8, 2002, must have completed at least 2 years of study at an IHE *or* earned an associate's degree or higher *or* met a rigorous standard of quality that demonstrates, through a formal state or local academic assessment, their ability to assist in instructing (a) reading, language arts, writing, and mathematics, or (b) reading readiness, writing readiness, and mathematics readiness.

2. All paraeducators, no matter when they were employed, must have a high school diploma or its equivalent.

Changes in Teacher Roles and Responsibilities

Over the last 2 decades, there have been intensive efforts across the country to reform education practices and systems and to improve the quality of education. A redefinition of the traditionally recognized roles of teachers is one of the most significant outcomes of efforts to reform and improve the quality of education. Just as the term *teacher's aide* no longer describes the roles of paraeducators, the term *classroom teacher* no longer adequately describes the roles of teachers. As members of school-based management teams, teachers join with principals, parents, and other school staff to (a) identify the learning needs of students in "their schools"; (b) establish program priorities to meet the identified needs; and (c) decide how to allocate limited fiscal, personnel, and technological resources to achieve the program goals for all learners.

Teachers—whether they work in preschools or elementary, middle, or secondary schools; serve learners in inclusive general or special education and multilingual classrooms; or serve students through Title I or other programs—are now responsible for (a) planning lessons to meet the curriculum requirements for an entire class, (b) modifying the lessons to meet the needs of individual learners, (c) engaging learners in instructional activities, and (d) evaluating the effectiveness of the lessons. Table 1.1 provides an overview of teachers' roles in planning, providing, and assessing the effectiveness of instructional and other direct services for learners and their families.

Changes in Paraeducator Roles and Responsibilities

Whether paraeducators are new or experienced, it is important for them to clearly understand the differences between teachers' roles and their

Table 1.1
Roles of Teachers in the Instructional Process

Teachers are responsible for the following:

- Developing lesson plans to meet curriculum requirements and education objectives for all learners
- Adapting lessons, instructional methods, and curricula to meet the learning needs of individual students
- Developing behavior management and disciplinary plans
- Creating learner-centered, inclusive environments that respect the cultures, religions, lifestyles, and human rights of children, youth, parents, and staff
- Engaging learners in instructional activities
- Implementing district policies and procedures for protecting the health, safety, and well-being of learners and staff
- Involving parents in all aspects of their child's education
- Analyzing, with the assistance of other licensed (credentialed) professional personnel, results of standardized tests for assessing learner needs
- Developing functional (informal) assessment tools to document and evaluate learner progress and instructional needs

Note. Adapted from *Strengthening and Supporting Teacher and Paraeducator Teams: Guidelines for Paraeducator Roles, Supervision, and Preparation* (pp. 15–17), by A. L. Pickett, 1999, New York: National Resource Center for Paraprofessionals in Education, Center for Advanced Study in Education, Graduate Center, City University of New York. Copyright 1999 by National Resource Center for Paraprofessionals in Education. Adapted with permission.

roles as members of instructional teams. Although paraeducators will still perform clerical, monitoring, and other routine activities, in most of their assignments they may spend as much as 90% of their time assisting teachers in the delivery of instructional and other direct services for learners and their parents (Fafard, 1974; Moshoyannis, Pickett, & Granik, 1999; Passaro, Pickett, Lathem, & HongBo, 1994; Pickett & Granik, 2003; SPeNSE Fact Sheet, 2001).

Although paraeducators participate in many instructional activities, their responsibilities are not the same as teachers'. What primarily distinguishes the responsibilities of teachers and paraeducators are the teacher roles that *may not* be delegated to paraeducators. Teachers (a) identify the learning needs and goals for all students, (b) plan lessons to meet those identified needs, (c) modify instructional strategies to meet the needs of individual learners, (d) evaluate the effectiveness of the instruction with regard to learner progress, and (e) involve parents in their child's education.

Paraeducators assist teachers in achieving the learning goals for children and youth by carrying out tasks developed by and assigned to them by teachers. For example, paraeducators *assist teachers* with implementing district policies and procedures for protecting the health, safety, and well-being of learners and staff members. Paraeducators *assist teachers* in providing individual or small-group instruction, following plans developed by the teacher. Paraeducators *assist teachers* in involving parents in their child's education. Paraeducators *assist teachers* with documenting information about learner performance. Table 1.2 shows the responsibilities carried out by paraeducators that support the different program and classroom management functions of teachers (Pickett & Safarik, 2003).

Changes in paraeducator roles have also come about because of an increased need for personnel who understand the cultures and speak the language of English language learners and their families. Many paraeducators live in the community served by the school where they work and come from the same ethnic and cultural backgrounds as the learners and their families. As a result, bilingual paraeducators frequently serve as mentors to help teachers and other school personnel understand how different cultural traditions, religious beliefs, and value systems might influence the learning preferences and communication styles of children and youth. Bilingual paraeducators may also provide translation services for school professionals, students, and their families.

Table 1.2

Roles of Paraeducators in the Instructional Process

Working under the direction of teachers, paraeducators are responsible for the following:

- Engaging individual and small groups of learners in instructional activities developed by teachers

- Helping to facilitate the inclusion of children and youth with disabilities into general education classrooms and programs

- Carrying out behavior management and disciplinary plans developed by teachers

- Documenting information that enables teachers to plan or modify lessons and adapt instructional methods to accommodate the learning and language needs of individual children and youth

- Assisting teachers with functional assessment activities

- Assisting teachers with maintaining inclusive learner-centered environments that respect the human rights, cultures, religions, and lifestyles of students and their families and of staff members

- Assisting teachers with carrying out district policies that protect the safety, health, and well-being of students and staff members and their learning environments

- Assisting teachers with involving families in their child's education

- Performing clerical and monitoring tasks assigned by the teacher (e.g., inventorying supplies, preparing instructional materials)

Note. Adapted from *Strengthening and Supporting Teacher and Paraeducator Teams: Guidelines for Paraeducator Roles, Supervision, and Preparation* (pp. 24–27), by A. L. Pickett, 1999, New York: National Resource Center for Paraprofessionals in Education, Center for Advanced Study in Education, Graduate Center, City University of New York. Copyright 1999 by National Resource Center for Paraprofessionals in Education. Adapted with permission.

Although this chapter does not focus on the growing demands for therapy and other related services for children and youth with physical and sensory disabilities, communication disorders, and health-related needs, paraeducators often work with occupational and physical therapists, speech–language pathologists, and nurses. The supervisory relationship between paraeducators and related services personnel (e.g., physical therapist) is similar to that between paraeducators and teachers.

Professional, Ethical, and Legal Responsibilities of Paraeducators

As key members of education teams, paraeducators have special relationships with teachers and other school personnel, learners, families, and members of their communities. The effectiveness of these relationships depends not only on their ability to carry out assigned tasks in a professional manner but also on their understanding of the ethical and legal requirements of their job. Demonstrating respect for the human rights of learners, their families, their teachers, and other colleagues; maintaining the confidentiality of all information connected to students and their families; following district policies and procedures; being dependable and cooperative; and participating in opportunities for training and career development are just a few of the areas in which paraeducators have professional, ethical, and legal obligations or responsibilities (Heller & Gerlach, 2003). Table 1.3 contains an outline of the professional, ethical, and legal responsibilities of paraeducators.

District Administrator, Principal, and Teacher Management Responsibilities

District administrators are responsible overall for ensuring that policies and personnel practices are established for the employment, preparation, and supervision of paraeducators. Principals are responsible for creating school environments that support and recognize the value of teacher and paraeducator teams and seeing that district policies and practices are carried out. Teachers are responsible for developing plans that fully tap the resources of paraeducators and for directing their work to effectively integrate them into the instructional process. (Tables 1.4 and 1.5 show distinctions of the responsibilities of administrators and principals.)

Mandates in NCLB and guidelines in IDEA recognize the need for teachers to participate in directing and monitoring the day-to-day work of paraeducators. Teachers have several supervisory responsibilities (described in Table 1.6) that effectively involve paraeducators in instruction and other classroom activities.

Table 1.3

Professional, Ethical, and Legal Responsibilities of Paraeducators

Paraeducator team members are responsible for the following:

- Practicing standards of professional and ethical conduct approved by the school district

- Respecting the legal and human rights of children, youth, their families, and school staff

- Performing tasks only for which they are trained

- Recognizing and respecting distinctions in the roles of teachers, other professional practitioners, and paraeducators

- Performing assigned tasks under the direction of teachers in a manner consistent with guidelines established by the SEAs, LEAs, or professional organizations representing different areas of education and related services

- Carrying out instructional activities, behavior management plans, and other tasks that are planned, modified, and assessed by teachers

- Sharing information with parents about their child's performance as directed by the supervising teacher

- Following LEA procedures for maintaining the confidentiality of written and oral records concerned with learner's academic performance and progress, results of formal and informal tests, behaviors, lifestyles, health and medical history, and other information about students and their families

- Sharing confidential information only with supervising teachers or other designated staff

- Not using language or actions that discriminate against learners, their families, and staff members based on differences in ability, race, culture, lifestyles, religion, or sex

- Following guidelines established by the school district to protect the health, safety, and well-being of learners and staff members

- Following the chain of command established by the district to address policy questions, systems issues, and personnel practices; when problems cannot be resolved, following the district's grievance procedure

- Participating with administrators and other stakeholders in creating and implementing opportunities for career development and advancement linked to identified skills and knowledge required by paraeducators

- Participating in opportunities for continuing education

Note. Adapted from "Professional and Ethical Responsibilities of Team Members," by W. Heller and K. Gerlach, 2003, in A. L. Pickett and K. Gerlach (Eds.), *Supervising Paraeducators in Education Settings: A Team Approach* (pp. 289–323), Austin, TX: PRO-ED. Copyright 2003 by PRO-ED, Inc. Adapted with permission.

Table 1.4

Responsibilities of District Administrators for the Management,
Supervision, and Preparation of Paraeducators

District-level administrators are responsible for the following:

- Developing standards for the employment, preparation, supervision, assessment, and dismissal of paraeducators

- Defining the roles of teachers in directing and monitoring the day-to-day work of paraeducators

- Developing performance standards for paraprofessionals

- Developing job descriptions for paraprofessionals that (a) recognize differences in teacher and paraeducator roles and responsibilities, (b) include core skills needed by all paraeducators and recognize differences in skills required to carry out tasks in various paraeducator positions, and (c) include pre- and in-service training and experiential requirements

- Providing opportunities for ongoing in-service competency-based training for paraeducators

- Working with 2- and 4-year IHEs to develop opportunities for career advancement for paraeducators whose personal goals are to earn AA degrees or teacher credentials

- Negotiating contractual agreements that include salaries, benefits, job descriptions, employment and education requirements, and reasons for dismissal

- Recruiting applicants for paraeducator positions

Note. Adapted from "Paraeducators in Education Settings: Administrative Issues," by S. Vasa, A. Steckelberg, and A. L. Pickett, 2003, in A. L. Pickett and K. Gerlach (Eds.), *Supervising Paraeducators in Education Settings: A Team Approach* (pp. 289–324), Austin, TX: PRO-ED. Copyright 2003 by PRO-ED, Inc. Adapted with permission.

Standards for Paraeducator Preparation and Supervision

In most states, standards and policies for paraeducator preparation and supervision are still not in place. Decisions about how to carry out the provisions in NCLB and IDEA are usually made in isolation, without consulting with paraeducators and teachers, or with the assistance and

Table 1.5

Roles of Principals in the Management of Paraeducators

Principals are responsible for the following:

- Implementing district policies and personnel practices connected with the employment, preparation, supervision, and dismissal of paraeducators

- Creating school environments that recognize the contributions that all staff members make to the delivery of effective education for all learners

- Interviewing candidates for paraeducator positions and, when possible, including teachers in the selection process

- Evaluating the overall performances of paraeducators and their supervising teachers

- Ensuring that teachers and paraeducators are aware of the differences in their roles and responsibilities

- Ensuring that teachers understand their responsibilities in directing and monitoring the day-to-day work of paraeducators

- Scheduling regular times for teachers and paraeducators to meet and discuss learner goals, plans for achieving those goals, and assignments for paraeducators; and providing opportunities for teachers to provide feedback and on-the-job training for paraeducators

- Ensuring that teachers and paraeducators are aware of and are able to follow district and school procedures for protecting the safety, health, and well-being of learners and staff members

- Sharing information with paraeducators about training opportunities; resource materials; state and national conferences concerned with issues of interest to them; changes in LEA or SEA policies that affect their employment, job descriptions, training, salaries, and benefits; and extracurricular activities and social events for staff members, students, and families

- Sharing information with teachers about training and materials that enhance their ability to effectively integrate paraeducators into instructional teams

Note. Adapted from "Paraeducators in Education Settings: Administrative Issues," by S. Vasa, A. Steckelberg, and A. L. Pickett, 2003, in A. L. Pickett and K. Gerlach (Eds.), *Supervising Paraeducators in Education Settings: A Team Approach* (pp. 255–288), Austin, TX: PRO-ED. Copyright 2003 by PRO-ED, Inc. Adapted with permission.

Table 1.6
Supervisory Responsibilities of Teachers

Supervising teachers are responsible for the following:

- Planning work assignments for paraeducators based on program objectives, learner needs, and the readiness of paraeducators to perform the task

- Developing daily and weekly schedules for paraeducators

- Planning and delegating noninstructional activities to paraeducators (e.g., inventorying supplies, filing information, reproducing instructional materials, reviewing parental permission forms for participating in field trips)

- Monitoring and documenting the day-to-day performance of paraeducators

- Providing feedback and on-the-job training to effectively integrate paraeducators into the instructional process and the team

- Sharing relevant information with principals about the strengths and any additional training paraeducators may require

Note. Adapted from: *Strengthening and Supporting Teacher and Paraeducator Teams: Guidelines for Paraeducator Roles, Supervision, and Preparation* (pp. 18–21), by A. L. Pickett, 1999, New York: National Resource Center for Paraprofessionals in Education, Center for Advanced Study in Education, Graduate Center, City University of New York. Copyright 1999 by National Resource Center for Paraprofessionals in Education. Adapted with permission.

support of the SEA, 2- and 4-year IHEs, unions, and other stakeholders. Thus structured, standardized career development programs, which include credentialing and opportunities for advancement, are almost nonexistent; if they do exist, often neither preservice nor in-service training is part of statewide systems of personnel development.

Because little attention has been paid to the issues surrounding the employment, roles, preparation, and supervision of paraeducators, it is important for SEAs, LEAs, and IHEs to join forces with paraeducators and teachers, advocacy and professional organizations, unions, and other stakeholders to assess current policies and standards in their state and identify statewide needs connected with establishing permanent training and career development programs for paraeducators. Such programs must (a) include systems to certify that paraeducators have mastered the skills required for their positions; (b) provide opportunities for advancement that recognize the need for higher levels of skills required by paraeducators working in more challenging positions, such as a job coach; and (c) provide access to 2- and 4-year IHE programs that take into account the needs of paraeducators who must work full-time while they earn a degree or certificate.

Summary

As always, educators must respond to and serve as agents for change. Policy makers and those who implement change are confronted with a multitude of problems as they seek more effective methods to improve the quality of America's schools. Among the more important but unrecognized issues is the need for policies, personnel practices, and systems to improve the performance of teacher and paraeducator teams. The roles and responsibilities of both teachers and paraeducators have changed dramatically over the last 50 years. However, few efforts are under way across the country to establish policies and systems to support and strengthen the performance of teacher and paraeducator teams. Establishing policies and programs to address the wide range of issues that impact the effectiveness of instructional teams is not an easy task and cannot be achieved by a single agency or organization. Cooperation among stakeholders—including teachers and paraeducators, SEA and LEA administrators, personnel developers in 2- and 4-year IHEs, unions, and professional organizations representing different areas of education personnel—is essential.

There are indications that demands for highly skilled paraeducators will continue. Growing numbers of students will come from families who live in poverty and other backgrounds that place them "at risk." The number of English language learners who come from different cultural and language heritages will continue to increase. All of these students—as well as those who have learning, physical, and other disabilities—benefit from individualized education and support services enhanced by the availability of skilled paraeducators. Establishing policies and programs that will enhance the effectiveness of teacher and paraeducator teams cannot be achieved in isolation by a single agency. There is only one course of action that will succeed—*we must all work together.*

ACTIVITIES

1. Depending on the size of your class, work in small groups of five or six or as a single group.

- Develop a list of the most significant factors that caused administrators to turn to paraeducators to assist teachers in the delivery of instructional and other direct services.
- Identify individuals in your LEA or community who are familiar with how the programs offered by the district have changed since paraeducators were introduced into classrooms.
- Set up interviews to determine whether various court-ordered mandates, federal legislation, and changes in learning- and language-related needs of the children and youth enrolled in the district's schools led to increased employment of paraeducators and changes in their responsibilities. (Because you will be covering events and issues that have developed over several years, it may be necessary to reach out to school board members; current and former district employees, including administrators, principals, teachers, and paraeducators; or parents of children and youth who have disabilities or who come from different ethnic, cultural, and language backgrounds.)
- As a group, prepare a written report to share with other members of the class.

2. Again, depending on the size of the class, divide into small groups or work as a single group to gather information about the following:

- state laws, written policies, and standards for the roles, training, and supervision of paraeducators, credentialing procedures, or other systems that enable paraeducators to demonstrate they have mastered the skills required for their positions
- community college programs for paraeducators in your community that offer certificate or AA degree programs for paraeducators
- your LEA's contracts with teachers and paraeducators
- personnel practices that affect the instructional, professional, legal, and ethical responsibilities, preparation, and supervision of paraeducators.

To gather this information you may have to use several resources, beginning with the Web sites for your SEA and LEA. If the information is not available on the Web sites, contact the LEA office of human resource and the SEA and LEA directors of Title I, special education, and other programs, and local community colleges. Other sources of information are contained in the Appendix at the end of the book. Review the various documents to determine if the following have occurred:

- Distinctions in teacher and paraeducator roles have been defined by either the SEA or your LEA
- Skill standards for paraeducator roles and responsibilities have been established by the SEA or your LEA that reflect the personnel development goals of IDEA or NCLB
- Employment and education requirements are established by the SEA or your LEA
- The SEA or your LEA has adopted or developed an academic assessment instrument that enables paraeducators to demonstrate they meet the skill standards
- The SEA has a credentialing system for paraeducators, either mandatory or voluntary (e.g., LEAs may determine whether or not to recognize the standards or procedures)
- There are community colleges in your area that offer either a certificate or an AA degree program for paraeducators
- Your SEA or LEA has established standards for the supervision of paraeducators; and the roles of teachers as directors and monitors of day-to-day performance are recognized
- The SEA or another agency responsible for teacher licensure has developed or adapted curriculum content to prepare teachers for directing and working effectively with paraeducators

3. Working together, use the results of your interviews and the analysis of the documents to identify the most important issues that require the attention of your SEA or LEA. Prepare a report to increase stakeholders' awareness of the need to ensure that paraeducators are highly skilled and that their day-to-day work is appropriately directed and monitored.

4. Work alone or with a small group, using Worksheet 1.1, Teacher and Paraeducator Role Perception Activity, to identify distinctions in teacher and paraeducator roles and responsibilities. Answer the following questions:

- What are the responsibilities of teachers that may not be delegated to paraeducators?
- What are the responsibilities of teachers that may be shared with paraeducators?

- Are there any responsibilities that only paraeducators should perform?

Discussion Questions

1. In the 1950s, what were the most significant events and other reasons that caused LEAs to turn to teacher's aides to provide support for teachers?

2. Why did the employment of paraeducators expand so dramatically in the 1960s and 1970s?

3. What effects have the changes in teachers' roles and responsibilities had on the roles and responsibilities of paraeducators?

4. What are the primary differences in the roles of district administrators, principals, and teachers in the management and supervision of paraeducators?

5. What are the primary instructional responsibilities of teachers?

6. In your state, are the differences in teachers' and paraeducators' roles clearly defined by either your SEA or LEA?

7. Are there statewide standards for the employment, roles, preparation, and supervision of paraeducators?

8. Does your state have a credentialing or other method to ensure that paraeducators have mastered the skills required to carry out their responsibilities?

9. Are there opportunities for training and career development in your state or LEA that recognize the needs of paraeducators who must work full-time while they earn a certificate, earn an AA degree, or participate in an advanced degree program?

References

Brown v. Board of Education, 374 U.S. 483 (1954).

Cruickshank, W., & Haring, N. (1957). *Assistants for teachers of exceptional children.* Syracuse, NY: Syracuse University Press.

Education for All Handicapped Children Act of 1975, U.S.C. 20 § 1400 *et seq.*

Elementary and Secondary Education Act of 1965, U.S.C. 79 stat.27.

Fafard, M. B. (1974). *Paraprofessionals in special education: The state of the art.* New York: New Careers Training Laboratory.

Ford Foundation, Fund for the Advancement of Education, 1951–61. (1961). *Decade of experiment.* New York: Author.

Gartner, A. (1971). *Paraprofessionals and their performance: A survey of education, health and social services programs.* New York: Praeger.

Heller, W., & Gerlach, K. (2003). Professional and ethical responsibilities of team members. In A. L. Pickett & K. Gerlach (Eds.), *Supervising paraeducators in education settings: A team approach* (pp. 289–324). Austin, TX: PRO-ED.

Individuals with Disabilities Education Act of 1997, 20 U.S.C. §1400 *et seq.*

Individuals with Disabilities Education Improvement Act of 2004, 20 U.S.C. §1400 *et seq.*

Kaplan, G. (1977). *From aide to teacher: The story of the career opportunities program.* Washington, DC: Government Printing Office.

Mills v. Board of Education of the District of Columbia, 348. Supp. 866 (DC, 1972).

Moshoyannis, T., Pickett, A. L., & Granik, L. (1999). *The evolving roles and education needs of paraprofessionals and teachers in the New York City public schools: Results of survey research and focus groups.* New York: City University of New York, Paraprofessional Academy, Center for Advanced Study in Education.

No Child Left Behind Act of 2001, U.S.C. § 2102 (4) 1119.

Passaro, P., Pickett, A. L., Lathem, G., & HongBo. (1994). The training and support needs of paraprofessionals in rural special education settings. *Rural Special Education Quarterly, 13*(4), 3–9.

Pennsylvania Association for Retarded Children v. the Commonwealth of Pennsylvania, 343 F. Supp. 279 (E.D. Pa.1972).

Pickett, A. L. (1989). *Restructuring the schools: The role of paraprofessionals.* Washington, DC: National Governors' Association, Center for Policy Research.

Pickett, A. L. (1999). *Strengthening and supporting teacher and paraeducator teams: Guidelines for paraeducators' roles, preparation, and supervision.* New York: National Resource Center for Paraprofessionals, Center for Advanced Study in Education, Graduate School, City University of New York.

Pickett, A. L., & Granik, L. (2003). *Factors related to paraprofessional roles, career development, and preparation.* Albany: New York State United Teachers.

Pickett, A. L., Likins, M., & Wallace, T. (2003). *A state-of-the-art report on paraeducators in education and related services.* Logan, UT: National Resource Center for Para-professionals.

Pickett, A. L., & Safarik, L. (2003). Team roles in classrooms and other learning environments. In A. L. Pickett & K. Gerlach (Eds.), *Supervising paraeducators in education settings: A team approach* (pp. 45–96). Austin, TX: PRO-ED.

Rehabilitation Act of 1973 (Section 504), 29 U.S.C. § 794.

SPeNSE Fact Sheet. (2001). *The roles of paraeducators in special education: Study of personnel needs in special education.* Available online from www.spense.org

Vasa, S., Steckelberg, A., & Pickett, A. L. (2003). Paraeducators in educational settings: Administrative issues. In A. L. Pickett & K. Gerlach (Eds.), *Supervising paraeducators in education settings: A team approach* (pp. 255–288). Austin, TX: PRO-ED.

WORKSHEET 1.1
Teacher and Paraeducator Role Perception Activity

Directions: Discuss the following tasks with the members of your group. When the group reaches consensus about whether a task should be performed exclusively by teachers or be shared with paraeducators, place an X in the appropriate box.

	Teacher	Shared
1. Recording and charting data about learner performance. . . .	☐	☐
2. Administering standardized tests.	☐	☐
3. Scoring standardized tests.	☐	☐
4. Grading tests and papers.	☐	☐
5. Analyzing and interpreting results of assessment activities . .	☐	☐
6. Evaluating learner performance	☐	☐
7. Setting goals and objectives for classes and individual learners	☐	☐
8. Planning lessons	☐	☐
9. Introducing new skills or concepts.	☐	☐
10. Modifying or adapting instructional plans for individual learners	☐	☐
11. Carrying out lesson plans	☐	☐
12. Instructing individual or small groups of learners	☐	☐
13. Developing behavior management plans	☐	☐
14. Implementing behavior management programs	☐	☐
15. Disciplining students.	☐	☐
16. Developing instructional materials	☐	☐
17. Recording attendance and maintaining other records	☐	☐
18. Setting up and maintaining learning centers and adaptive equipment.	☐	☐
19. Inventorying and ordering supplies	☐	☐
20. Participating in individualized program planning and other school-based meetings	☐	☐
21. Meeting and conferring with parents	☐	☐
22. Consulting with professional staff about learners' programs and behaviors	☐	☐
23. Maintaining a clean, safe learning environment	☐	☐

Teamwork, Communication, and Problem Solving

2

Kent Gerlach

• •

Team success and a positive working relationship depend on good communication. As Chapter 1 stated, paraeducators do not work in isolation; they work alongside teachers in supporting roles. For a teacher and paraeducator to work together, they must view themselves as a team and as partners in the educational process. The teacher and paraeducator must understand the importance of a working relationship that is built on good communication, teamwork, and mutual respect. Good teamwork requires effort, commitment, and a willingness to accept the challenges of working together.

Learning Objectives

The content of this chapter will prepare the paraeducator to do the following:

1. Define teamwork, communication, and problem solving
2. Identify communication skills for working with other team members
3. Understand the importance of listening appropriately
4. Explain the importance of problem solving as it applies to school-based teams
5. Identify and apply the eight-step problem-solving process
6. Identify and give examples of the types of strategies used to seek, provide, and clarify information
7. Describe the major purposes and importance of questions

8. Discuss the nature and possible sources of conflict among team members
9. Describe successful meetings and activities that contribute to their success

Key Terms and Definitions

The following key terms and definitions will be used throughout this chapter.

Collaboration. A process of joining together to work on tasks in a cooperative, respectful, and purposeful manner.

Collaborative education team. An instructional arrangement of two or more people in schools, communities, and agencies who share cooperative planning and instructional responsibilities for the same students on a regular basis (Howard, Williams, Port, & Lepper, 1994, p. 414).

Communication. The ability to share information with people and to understand the information and feelings conveyed by others. It is a process of exchanging information between the person who sends the message and the person who receives the message.

Listening. A process for attending to and accurately comprehending what another person is saying and then demonstrating that this happened.

Paraphrasing. An immediate response in which one restates what another person has said.

Perception checking. A process whereby one asks for clarification or confirmation that the restated content is accurate, usually combining a statement with a question.

Reflecting. The paraeducator restates what the teacher and others have said by using additional descriptive words to try to capture the feeling of what was said.

Summarizing. One or more statements that restate what another individual has said.

Team. Two or more people working together toward a common goal, mission, or purpose.

Teamwork

Teamwork can be defined as "a process among partners who share mutual goals and work together to achieve the goals." Teamwork allows people to discuss their responsibilities and, as a result, to grow professionally. Abelson and Woodman (1983) stressed that a "team" is two or more inter-dependent individuals who work together and communicate directly in a coordinated manner in order to reach an agreed-upon goal(s). Shared goals, good communication, role clarification, and clear direction are important for team success.

If a team is to be effective, members must acknowledge the benefits of working together.

1. Roles and responsibilities of both the teacher and paraeducator must be clearly defined and discussed.
2. The supervising teacher must clearly share expectations in order to get the jobs done.
3. The mission and goals of the team must be developed with input from all team members.
4. Information must be shared in a timely manner, and the team's meeting time should be effective and productive.
5. Scheduling a paraeducator's time to meet regularly with his or her supervising teacher is an important consideration for team success.

Effective communication allows team members to share their beliefs, ideas, needs, or feelings. Effective team performance is based on communication that allows for a free flow of ideas and information that contributes to shared understanding. When ideas are shared, there is opportunity for feedback and evaluation of input that can lead to even better ideas. From each new experience, more ideas can be developed and tried. Successful communication results in a mutual understanding of what is said and what is heard.

Trust: Essential for Team Success

Open communication, mutual respect, recognition, and, above all, trust serve as a foundation for building effective teams. Trust is shown by promoting open communication, providing fair leadership, and supervising with sensitivity (Pickett & Gerlach, 2003).

Trust is necessary for a productive working environment. It is essential for all team members to practice open, honest communication in order to increase awareness and to build cooperation. This environment of trust promotes loyalty and commitment to achieve the goals and objectives of the team.

Effective Teams Are Goal Focused

Because many paraeducators receive limited training or orientation for their jobs, it is especially important that the supervising teacher accurately and clearly describe the goals and needs of the learner being served. The best team members understand learner goals and how each person contributes to reaching them. Priorities are established much more easily when teams focus on goals. Together, the teacher, other professional practitioners, and the paraeducator determine what needs to be done, by whom, and by what deadline. Elements of a goal include (a) what will be achieved; (b) a measure of accomplishment (i.e., How will we know when the outcome has been reached?), and (c) the time factor (i.e., When precisely do we want to have the goal completed?). All team members must agree on the goals for their work. These efforts would also include supporting and mentoring one another.

Teachers and paraeducators need to be aware of and understand their roles in completing tasks, and teachers need to know how to use the skills and expertise of each member most effectively. Several factors must be considered in determining the roles and responsibilities of paraeducators, including the paraeducator's experience, training, comfort level, time constraints, and knowledge and skill levels. Professional and ethical considerations are important when determining roles for the paraeducator team. In other words, role clarification is a critical element for the success of the paraeducator–teacher team.

Effective leadership is critical for team success. The leader is always the teacher or another licensed or certified school professional who is designated as the paraeducator's supervisor. The supervisor's role is similar to that of a coach and involves assessing the paraeducator's skills and helping the paraeducator use them to the fullest. Paraeducators contribute more effectively when they are "coached" and encouraged to make optimal use of their strengths and resources. The supervising teacher provides direction and ideas, helps identify alternatives, raises questions, and supplies feedback (see Figure 2.1).

- Do all team members understand team goals?
- Are all team members committed to these goals?
- Are team members concerned and interested in each other?
- Do team members acknowledge and confront conflict openly?
- Do team members listen to each other with openness and understanding?
- Do all members value one another's contributions?
- Do team members feel comfortable contributing ideas and solutions?
- Do team members recognize and reward team performance?
- Do team members encourage and appreciate comments about team efforts?
- Are team meetings held at a specific time?
- Is leadership effective?
- Is constructive feedback given freely to improve decision making?
- Is information shared willingly?

Figure 2.1. Assess teacher and paraeducator effectiveness. *Note.* From "Teamwork: Key to Success for Teachers and Paraeducators," by K. Gerlach, 2002, *Impact, 15,* p. 11. Copyright 2004 by Kent Gerlach. Reprinted with permission.

The Supervisor as Mentor

Teacher-mentors share valuable knowledge and skills with paraeducators. Mentoring is a process that enables the teacher and paraeducator to work together to discover and develop the paraeducator's knowledge and skills as opportunities and needs arise.

According to Gerlach (2002), the teacher as a supervisor, mentor, and team leader

1. sets expectations of the paraeducator's performance;
2. offers challenging plans and ideas;
3. helps build the self-confidence of the paraeducator;
4. encourages ethical and professional behavior;
5. offers support;
6. listens actively;
7. leads and teaches by example;

8. asks questions and gives explanations to the paraeducator;
9. coaches the paraeducator;
10. encourages the paraeducator;
11. inspires the paraeducator;
12. shares critical knowledge;
13. assists, observes, and demonstrates effective instructional practice;
14. directs and delegates effectively to the paraeducator; and
15. gives clear, concise directions to the paraeducator.

Team Characteristics

The characteristics of successful teams can be found throughout the research literature for social services and business. A "team" is two or more people working toward a common goal, mission, or purpose (Gerlach, 2004c). By focusing on goals, priorities can be determined much more easily. Together, teachers and paraeducators decide what needs to be done, how it will be done, who will do it, and by what deadline. The paraeducator needs to know not only the goals for the team but also the goals for the students he or she might work with.

Teamwork does not happen by accident. Effective teamwork requires commitment, effort, and energy. When a paraeducator and teacher work well together, they can provide services they can be proud of to learners and families. This takes initiative, a willingness to accept the uniqueness of others, and a respect for diversity.

When the paraeducator and teacher work well together, many individual and group benefits emerge as a result of the process. Figure 2.2 lists the advantages of the team concept, and Figure 2.3 lists the characteristics of a successful team.

To create a positive teacher and paraeducator team, it is important to establish a climate that includes the following:

1. Team roles and responsibilities that are defined
2. Team members who feel that they are integral to the success of the team
3. A safe atmosphere for all team members to express feelings and ask questions
4. Each team member receiving recognition, acceptance, feedback, and appreciation

- Teams build an awareness of interdependence. When people recognize the benefits of helping one another and realize it is expected, they will work together to achieve common goals.

- When people work together to achieve common goals, they stimulate each other to higher levels of accomplishment; fresh ideas are generated.

- Teamwork builds and reinforces recognition and mutual support within a team. People have an opportunity to see the effect of their efforts and the efforts of others on student achievement.

- Good communication leads to the commitment to support and accomplish student and team goals.

- Teams develop unique, creative, and flexible solutions to problems.

- Teams foster professional and personal growth by sharing knowledge and skills.

- Teams reduce the feeling of isolation that is common in education.

- Teams support and mentor each other.

- Teams maximize each member's potential strengths and contribution.

- Teams establish goals together. Members feel a sense of ownership toward goals. Input is solicited from all team members.

- Members are encouraged to openly express ideas, opinions, disagreement, and feelings. Questions are welcomed.

- Team members practice open and honest communication. They make an effort to understand each other's points of view. They operate in a climate of trust and respect.

- Members participate in discussions affecting the team but understand that their supervisor or leader must make the final decision.

- A team spirit develops when members work well together.

Figure 2.2. Advantages of "the team" concept. *Note.* Adapted from *Supervising Paraeducators in Educational Settings: A Team Approach* (2nd ed., p. 174), by A. L. Pickett and K. Gerlach, 2003, Austin, TX: PRO-ED. Copyright 2003 by PRO-ED, Inc. Adapted with permission.

5. Respect for and acceptance of individual differences, educational differences, and cultural differences
6. Team members establishing helpful interpersonal relationships and mentoring one another

---

- Successful teams use their time and talents effectively.
- Successful teams are committed to skill development.
- Team members build morale by showing respect and recognition to one another.
- Team members give one another feedback.
- Team members cooperate rather than compete.
- Team members maintain positive attitudes toward each other's ideas.
- Successful teams communicate openly.
- Team members mentor and learn from one another.
- Successful teams resolve conflicts effectively.
- Successful teams accept challenges.

Figure 2.3. Characteristics of successful teams. *Note.* Adapted from *Supervising Paraeducators in Educational Settings: A Team Approach* (2nd ed., p. 174), by A. L. Pickett and K. Gerlach, 2003, Austin, TX: PRO-ED. Copyright 2003 by PRO-ED, Inc. Adapted with permission.

7. Support and concern expressed for one another
8. Team members being involved and giving input into the team process
9. Supports staff development
10. Establishes mutual trust and respect between the teacher and paraeducator

Communication

Effective communication is critical to the success of the team. An assessment of communication skills is now part of most performance reviews in the workplace.

Interpersonal Communication

Communication has been defined as the ability to share information with people and to understand the information and feelings being conveyed by others. As the roles of paraeducators have expanded and become more complex and challenging, the need for effective communication and problem-solving skills has also increased (Pickett, Faison, & Formanek, 1998). Effective communication skills are essential for a paraeducator to be a successful team member; effective communication and teamwork are critical in the performance of today's school personnel. Communication is a process of exchanging information between the sender and the receiver and includes a broad range of actions that help the paraeducator work more effectively with teachers, other team members, parents, families, and students. The information acts as the message (Trenholm, 2001). Ideas, feelings, and attitudes are communicated through gestures, facial expressions, tone of voice, and signs in addition to speech and written communication.

Open channels of communication are important for several reasons. By talking to the supervising teacher and other team members, paraeducators can convey any special interests, talents, training, or habits they might have that could be an asset to determining their roles in instruction and other classroom responsibilities.

Listening: Critical Element of Communication

All team members need to develop effective listening skills so that they can obtain sufficient and accurate information, which is necessary for effective team communication. Listening is a complex and difficult-to-measure process that involves attending to and accurately comprehending what another person is saying and then demonstrating that comprehension has occurred (Brammer & McDonald, 1999). Listening shows that one is interested in the message of others. Paraeducators gain needed information by listening to the supervising teacher and other team members. When paraeducators show good listening skills, they show a desire to understand the situation and what the speaker is saying. The following vignette demonstrates listening strategies.

> When Maria, the paraeducator, meets with her supervising teacher, Ellen, Maria mentally prepares for the meeting by directing her total attention to Ellen. She puts down all paperwork and materials, and eliminates all distractions as much as possible.
>
> Maria focuses on key words and the main message of the communication. She sometimes practices repeating these messages mentally as Ellen shares more information about the lesson plan. Maria categorizes

the information by making notes of informational details. She jots down important details pertaining to the lesson and to her role in assisting with instruction.

What are the effective listening strategies used in this case study?

Confirming and Clarifying Information

After listening, it is important to clarify the information that is being shared or stated. Typical methods to help clarify statements are summarizing, paraphrasing, checking, asking questions, and reflecting.

Summarizing

Summarizing is an important way to clarify what the other person said. Summarizing consists of one or more statements that pull together important facts or ideas and restate what an individual has said. It is a way of ensuring that everyone engaged in the conversation understands what is being said. Usually, summarization is a response to many pieces of information; it establishes a basis for further discussion. An example of a summary statement might be "These seem to be the main ideas."

Paraphrasing

Paraphrasing is usually an immediate response after listening to a series of statements. One example of this would be that the paraeducator restates what he or she thinks the teacher or supervisor has said. In the following example, Tina, a paraeducator, and Harold, the supervising teacher, are conferring on how to deal with a student's frequent outbursts in the classroom.

TINA: We have tried several strategies, but with little success.

HAROLD: I think we should record the number of times Danny (the student) has a temper outburst in class.

TINA: Do you want me to record every time he yells out in class?

HAROLD: Yes, and not only do we need to record the number of outbursts but also how long the outburst lasts.

TINA: Okay, you want me to record the number of temper outbursts and how long each one of them lasts.

HAROLD: Yes, will you be able to do that?

TINA: Yes, I will be able to record the number of times Danny has a temper outburst and how long it lasts. We can use that for a new plan.

By accurately restating the main points in the teacher's statements, the paraeducator demonstrated an understanding of what the teacher (Harold) was saying. Tina, the paraeducator, conveyed interest in the situation as well as in Harold (the teacher) as a person (see Figure 2.4 for a list of how paraeducators can clarify information).

Perception checking

In perception checking, the paraeducator checks for the accuracy of the information by combining a statement and a question. For example, Anne, the paraprofessional, and Bill, the teacher, have been discussing the lesson plan for small-group instruction. Bill shows Anne a teacher's guide to be used in the activity. An example of perception checking would be for Anne to say that she will follow the guide and then ask a question about the guide or activity: "This is a very detailed plan, where do I obtain the materials to follow the plan?"

Asking questions

Asking questions is perceived as a strength, not a weakness (see Figure 2.5). Paraeducators should use questions if an assignment is unclear

---

- **Summarizing**—After listening to a conversation, the paraeducator restates several main points said by the teacher.

- **Paraphrasing**—The paraeducator restates what the teacher has said, using many of the words used by the teacher.

- **Perception checking**—The paraeducator restates and asks for clarification or confirmation that the restated content is accurate and that others involved have similar perceptions of what was said.

- **Questioning**—The paraeducator should ask questions if he or she is not clear about his or her role.

- **Reflecting**—The paraeducator restates what the teacher or others have said by using additional descriptive words to try to capture the feelings of what was said.

Figure 2.4. Ways paraeducators can confirm and clarify information.

Why ask questions?
- It stimulates the other person to communicate with you.
- It seeks information.
- It broadens the discussion.
- It includes additional facts.
- It checks conclusions or challenges old ideas.
- It clarifies thinking.
- It develops new ideas.
- It offers alternatives.
- It facilitates decision making.
- It gains agreement.
- It obtains commitments to ensure responsibilities for accomplishing a task.

When formulating questions, keep these simple rules in mind:
- Make them short.
- Make them easily understood.
- Avoid leading questions.
- Avoid double questions.
- Use open questions.

Figure 2.5. Asking for assistance is a strength, not a weakness.

or not enough information is provided for them. Information gathering is important for team success. Questions provide a way of requesting more information, if needed. If not enough information is given about a student, a paraeducator should request information about a student's needs.

Asking questions is a good way to develop effective interpersonal problem solving to elicit pertinent information, and questions continue to be essential throughout the process for clarifying ideas and understanding. Skillful use of questions can mean the difference between an intervention that is successful and one that is fraught with miscommunications and parallel communication (Friend & Cook, 2003).

Phrasing a question in a positive, professional way is an important skill for all team members to have. Questions seek information, provide information, and clarify information. Examples of questions that seek information would be, "How many students will be in the group?" or "Which program do you feel would be best for the group?" An example of a question that provides information would be, "What do you think would happen if you asked the students' parents to assist us with the program?" An example of a question that clarifies information would be, "Are you saying that you prefer this new program to the one that we used last semester?"

Pausing is a key to effective questioning (Brammer & McDonald, 1999). It is important to pause before and after a question is asked; pausing is an important communication skill that takes practice to become effective. By carefully constructing questions to gain the information needed, the paraeducator can greatly contribute to effective team communication and be more comfortable with the role he or she plays in the instruction process.

Reflecting

By reflecting, a paraeducator describes what the teacher or other person has said and tries to state the meaning of the message. Reflecting demonstrates understanding of the other person's feelings, as the following illustrates:

TEACHER: I have so much to do and another meeting today. Sometimes I just feel like it is not worth the time to prepare these meetings [teacher sighs].

PARAEDUCATOR: You do have a lot on your plate today. You seem upset. Is there anything I can do to help you today?

In this vignette, the paraeducator restated the teacher's message in her own words and then stated her understanding of the situation. This response is very important in building team communication because it can promote a sense of respect and trust. It shows that the speaker's feelings are valued and that the listener understands how he or she feels.

Problem-Solving Strategies

Problem-solving skills are important for successful team interaction. Many of the duties, tasks, and activities for which a paraeducator is responsible involve some type of problem. Therefore, the ability to problem solve is fundamental to successful interactions with supervising teachers and other team members.

Many authors (e.g., Dewey, 1993; Fishbaugh, 2000; Pickett & Gerlach, 2003; Snell & Janney, 2000) have identified approaches to effective problem solving. A nine-step problem-solving process applies strategies from the various authors and sources:

1. Identify and define the problem
2. Define and determine the cause of the problem
3. Determine the needs and desired results
4. Brainstorm possible solutions
5. Select the solution that will best meet the needs
6. Develop a plan of action
7. Implement the plan
8. Evaluate the solution and problem-solving process
9. Respond to conflict

By using these steps to identify problems and develop ideas to solve them, paraeducators will learn how the team's work can be strengthened.

Identify and Define the Problem

A situation must be clearly understood before it can be dealt with. Research reveals that (a) problem identification is the most important step in problem solving (Jayanthi & Friend, 1992; Pickett & Gerlach, 2003; Welch & Tulbert, 2000), and (b) the remainder of the strategy will be successful if the problem has been accurately delineated (Bergan & Tombari, 1975). It is not always easy to put a problem into words, but if it cannot be stated clearly it will be impossible to choose a course of action that will lead to a satisfactory solution.

Asking and answering questions helps promote development of a shared understanding of the problem. Team members describe the problem based on their point of view. Each person should answer the following questions by describing the problem in his or her own words and point of view.

1. What is the problem?
2. What is not working in this situation?
3. What factors are contributing to this problem?
4. Who is involved (students, staff, family)?
5. Who is affected and how?

The teacher and paraeducator should individually consider these questions and prepare answers to be used in decisions. Once all team members have contributed to identifying the problem, the team can draft a problem statement. This process brings the team to a consensus about the problem.

Determine the Cause of the Problem

It is not enough to just identify the problem; it is also essential to determine what causes the problem to exist and persist. For example, the problem may be caused by "outside conditions" (contractual agreements, a lack of financial resources) that the team may have little ability to change, or it may result from a lack of understanding of the distinction in the roles and duties of the teacher and paraeducator. Other factors that may influence how a problem is defined include differences in values and attitudes, age, work experience and education, cultural heritage, and other personal traits. It is important that the team identify those areas of agreement and disagreement (Pickett & Gerlach, 2003).

Determine the Needs and Desired Results

Questions that should be asked to determine the needs and desired results of a problem include, "What are the desired results?" "What is needed to make this happen?" "What is needed to improve our communication with all of those involved?" The team can focus on what it wants to achieve by answering these and other questions.

Brainstorm Possible Solutions

For brainstorming to generate solutions to the problem-solving process, members of the team must agree on the following brainstorming rules:

1. Establish a time frame
2. Propose ideas freely
3. Accept all ideas offered
4. Do not evaluate ideas at this time
5. Write ideas on paper or use a computer
6. Make sure all team members participate

A good brainstorming session will probably produce several ideas to help solve problems.

Select the Solution That Will Best Meet the Needs

The team needs to consider the positives and negatives of each potential solution and outline the responsibilities of each team member who is needed to implement the solution. Additional questions to be asked include, "Which solution will meet the needs and achieve the desired results?" "Which solution can be managed by the team?" "Which solution would be easiest to implement?" Discussions of these or similar questions will help to identify a solution that will be acceptable to all team members.

Develop a Plan of Action

Everyone on the team needs to know what must be done and by whom. A written action plan provides a way for clarifying these roles in achieving the goals of the plan. An action plan could include a description of the task, the person(s) responsible, the expected outcomes, the date for completion, and a place for comments or evaluation.

Implement the Plan

Role clarification is important for determining who is responsible for the different components of the plan (Gerlach, 2004b). Other items for discussion would include a schedule change, resources, meeting times, and communication with others about the plan. The team must try it out and test it to see if the plan will work.

Evaluate the Results

The team needs to determine whether the plan effectively achieved the results desired. Has the problem been resolved? Is there progress? If not, why not? Should the team try other alternatives? After analyzing the results, the team should review the problem-solving process and determine how well it worked. On the basis of the results, the team will need to decide to continue, make adaptations as necessary, or, if a step in the process did not work, determine where the process broke down. The use of this mutual problem-solving process fosters cooperative working partnerships between school professionals and paraeducators and results in better services for students and families.

Respond to Conflict

The team may encounter conflicts that are influenced significantly by the organization and administration of the school (Goldman, 1998; Kosmoski & Pollack, 2000). Conflict occurs in any working relationship. In education settings, conflicts may arise at any point. Education personnel working together may experience conflict as a result of opposing ideas, unclear goals, or confusion over roles or behavior management strategies. For example, a teacher and a paraeducator might have different beliefs about the level of support a student needs to be integrated successfully into the general education classroom. The teacher might feel that the student needs to do his work more independently, whereas the paraeducator feels he is not ready for independent work. The teacher feels the paraeducator is hanging over the student and assisting him more than necessary. When such disagreement occurs, it is important that the conflict is resolved. In problem solving, a series of steps called "conflict resolution strategies" should be followed (see Figure 2.6).

Step 1: Pause and reflect

Step 2: Identify the conflict or source of the conflict

Step 3: Determine what part you play in the conflict

Step 4: Determine the various options

Step 5: Choose the best option or strategy

Step 6: Develop an action plan

Figure 2.6. Conflict resolution strategy. *Note.* Adapted from *Supervising Paraeducators in Educational Settings: A Team Approach* (2nd ed., p. 92), by A. L. Pickett and K. Gerlach, 2003, Austin, TX: PRO-ED. Copyright 2003 by PRO-ED, Inc. Adapted with permission.

◆ *Step 1: Pause and reflect.* The first step in resolving conflict is to step back and think about the situation. This will give each person a new perspective and prevent the conflict from escalating.

◆ *Step 2: Identify the conflict.* It is important to recognize what the source of the conflict is. Recognizing the source of conflict must be done in a thoughtful manner; thus there is a better chance that the resolution will be effective and that the conflict will be addressed.

◆ *Step 3: Determine what part you play in the conflict.* Thomas and Kilmann (1974) identified five typical responses to conflict: avoidance, accommodating, compromise, competition, and collaboration. Each of these responses can contribute to productive conflict resolution. This is the time for individuals involved in the conflict to analyze their part in it.

◆ *Step 4: Determine the various options.* It is necessary to determine the alternatives available and to consider and evaluate the potential for success offered by the different options. The team can then decide if they should let things continue, address the issue with those involved, develop a new way of thinking about the conflict, or use the problem-solving approach discussed earlier.

◆ *Step 5: Choose the best option or strategy.* After an evaluation by which the team analyzes the benefits and strengths, liabilities, or weaknesses of the different choices, the team would choose the one most likely to resolve the conflict effectively.

◆ *Step 6: Develop an action plan.* Plan to take whatever steps are necessary to implement your choice. Putting the plan into action is the final and most important step.

If the team follows these six steps, it is possible for the conflict to be resolved, and the result will be a more trusting and respectful approach for dealing with conflicts.

Meeting with Your Supervisor

A major obstacle to effective teamwork for teachers and paraeducators is the lack of planning time available in a daily or weekly schedule. It is important that the teacher and paraeducator find time in the weekly schedule to meet together. Teachers and paraeducators who work in self-contained special education classes may combine their breaks and planning times. If the paraeducator works in an inclusion program or in a different classroom, however, he or she must find another solution. It is important that paraeducators (a) attend regularly scheduled meetings called by their supervisors, (b) be punctual, (c) come prepared for the meeting, (d) think about questions ahead of time and ask questions if they are unclear about the instruction, (e) contribute to meeting goals, and (f) respect the confidentiality of students and families.

Summary

In today's education climate, the most successful schools operate as a team. School personnel understand the importance of good communication, a good working relationship, and the focus on team goals. When teachers and paraeducators communicate, students are the ultimate beneficiaries (Gerlach, 2004a). More than ever before, children need to see adults working well together. Good communication, teamwork, and problem-solving strategies will benefit everyone.

ACTIVITIES

1. Now that you have completed this chapter, how do you plan to share the information you have learned with your colleagues (administration, teachers, paraeducators, others)? One way would be to develop a Team Action Plan:

- Decide what you want to (need to) do in order to improve a team performance (problem identification and goal).

- How will this improve the organization and operation of your team?
- Describe some of the steps (solutions) you will use to achieve your objective.
- Decide where, when, and how you will implement the solution you select.

2. Discuss a communication situation or a meeting you attended that was difficult for you. Discuss the reasons for that difficulty. List ways you would improve the situation the next time it occurs.

3. List some of the obstacles faced by school personnel regarding time for communication and planning. What needs to happen to improve the situation?

4. List characteristics of effective teams. What do you feel is most important for team success?

5. If you have worked in a setting in which teamwork was valued and encouraged, write a summary of your experience. Use this as the basis for a discussion with others to generate specific examples of the characteristics of teamwork and effective communication.

6. List the teams of which you are a member or have been a member. Consider which teams were most effective and why.

7. Think of a problem about a student that a teacher has mentioned to you. Imagine an interaction in which you assist the teacher to help solve the problem.

8. Think about possible questions paraeducators might ask regarding lesson plans given to them by supervising teachers.

9. Think about a conflict that you have recently experienced. How did you resolve the conflict, or how do you plan to resolve the conflict in the future based on what you have learned from this chapter?

10. List the stages in the problem-solving process. Set up a role-playing

situation in which a problem is identified. Develop a role-play that uses the problem-solving process.

11. Think about conflicts you have experienced in your personal life or in a work situation. How were these conflicts resolved? Now that you know about problem-solving and conflict-resolution strategies, explain how you would handle things, the same or differently.

12. Identify two issues that school personnel might encounter in which the problem-solving or conflict-resolution strategy could be used.

Discussion Questions

1. Regarding supervision, what skills are necessary to direct and manage the work of paraeducators? What should a paraeducator expect from a teacher concerning teamwork and communication?

2. What should a teacher expect from a paraeducator concerning teamwork and communication?

3. When someone delegates to you, or when someone asks you to do something, what are some of the things you most appreciate (e.g., clear, concise direction)?

4. What is the importance of a positive school environment, and how does an effective paraeducator and teacher team enhance this learning environment?

5. Why are the following important for good communication and team effectiveness?

   - Following a written agenda to make sure team meetings are productive
   - Setting aside a regular time period for meeting with your supervising teacher
   - Discussing goals, objectives, priorities, and plans with your supervising teacher
   - Making sure expectations are reasonable and clear
   - Providing complete information and clear instructions (i.e., make sure team members understand everything and the importance of deadlines)
   - Developing an ongoing dialogue on how best to use team time

References

Abelson, M. A., & Woodman, R. W. (1983). Review of research on team effectiveness: Implications for teams in schools. *School Psychology Review, 12*(2), 125–136.

Bergan, J. R., & Tombari, M. L. (1975). The analysis of verbal instructions occurring during consultation. *Journal of School Psychology, 13*, 209–226.

Brammer, L. M., & MacDonald, G. (1999). *The helping relationship profess and skills* (7th ed.). Boston: Allyn & Bacon.

Dewey, J. (1993). *How we think*. Boston: Heath.

Fishbaugh, M. S. E. (2000). *The collaboration guide for early career educators*. Baltimore: Brookes.

Friend, M., & Cook, L. (2003). *Interactions: Collaboration skills for school professionals* (4th ed.). White Plains, NY: Longman.

Gerlach, K. (2002, Fall). Teamwork: Key to success for teachers and paraeducators. *Impact, 15*, 10–11.

Gerlach, K. (2004a). *Let's team up! A checklist for paraeducators, teachers, and principals (NEA checklist series)*. Washington, DC: National Education Association.

Gerlach, K. (2004b). *The paraeducator and teacher team: Strategies for success, roles, responsibilities and ethical issues*. Seattle, WA: Pacific Training Associates.

Gerlach, K. (2004c). *The paraeducator and teacher team: Strategies for success, communication and team building*. Seattle, WA: Pacific Training Associates.

Goldman, E. (1998). The significance of leadership style. *Educational Leadership, 55*(7), 20–22.

Howard, V. F., Williams, B. F., Port, P. D., & Lepper, C. (1994). *Very young children with special needs: A formative approach for the 21st century*. Upper Saddle River, NJ: Merrill.

Jayanthi, M., & Friend, M. (1992). Interpersonal problem solving: A selected literature review to guide practice. *Journal of Educational and Psychological Consultation, 3*, 147–152.

Kosmoski, G. J., & Pollack, D. R. (2000). *Managing difficulty, frustrations, and hostile conversations: Strategies for savvy administrators*. Thousand Oaks, CA: Corwin.

Pickett, A. L., Faison, K., & Formanek, J. (1998). *A core curriculum and training program to prepare paraeducators to work in inclusive classrooms serving school age students with disabilities* (2nd ed.). New York: National Resource Center for Advanced Study in Education and Related Services.

Pickett, A. L., & Gerlach, K. P. (2003). *Supervising paraeducators in school settings: A team approach*. Austin, TX: PRO-ED.

Snell, M. E., & Janney, R. (2000). *Collaborative teaming*. Baltimore: Brookes.

Thomas, K., & Kilmann, R. (1974). *Thomas-Kilmann, Conflict Mode Instrument*. Tuxedo, NY: Xicon.

Trenholm, S. (2001). *Thinking through communication: An introduction to the study of human communication* (3rd ed.). Boston: Allyn & Bacon.

Welch, M., & Tulbert, B. (2000). Practitioners' perspectives of collaboration: A social validation and factor analysis. *Journal of Educational and Psychological Consultation, 11,* 357–378.

Exploring the Roles of the Paraeducator in Instruction

3

Robert Morgan

With effective training and supervision, paraeducators become valuable team members who actively participate in monitoring and delivering instruction to learners in classrooms. First, this chapter examines the paraeducator's roles in instruction; second, it describes methods the paraeducator can use to deliver effective instruction; third, it warns of excessive prompting, or "taking over"; and fourth, it considers the paraeducator's role in lesson plans, instructional settings, management, groupings, and assessment of learning style.

Learning Objectives

The content of this chapter will prepare paraeducators to do the following:

1. Describe the paraeducator's roles in instruction (e.g., observer, data collector, monitor, trained assistant in delivering instruction).
2. Describe the use of validated instructional practices across settings and instructional groupings (e.g., one-on-one instruction, small-group instruction).
3. Identify procedures to use and to avoid in prompting learners to perform tasks.
4. Understand the impact of different learning styles and preferences on the performance of individual children and youth.

Key Terms and Definitions

The following key terms and definitions will be used throughout this chapter.

Curriculum-based assessment (CBA). Taking samples from curriculum areas to create an assessment to pinpoint the level of learning for an individual child

Data collection. Observing and recording information on a learner's performance

Generalization. Performing a learned skill with a different person, in a different place, or with new materials

Goal. A general measurable performance standard

Guided practice. Guiding the learner in practicing a response

Independent practice. Watching the learner perform a response without assistance

Informal assessments. Tests of a learner's performance in an academic, social, or other skill area (such as a CBA) that provide information about strengths and weaknesses

Modality. The method or medium for learning, such as visual, auditory, or touch

Model or demonstration. Showing or telling the learner what to do

Physical prompting. A form of temporary help in performing motor activities, such as basic self-help skills

Prelesson review. A brief assessment of previously learned skills

Short-term objective. Measurable performance standards arranged in sequence to meet a goal

The Learning Process

Learning is a process involving a learner who is guided by someone more skilled (such as a teacher or paraeducator) towards achieving a preset performance standard. A general measurable performance standard is called a "goal" (Snell & Brown, 2000). Goals may be divided into several short-term objectives or into smaller measurable performance standards arranged in sequence to meet the goal. Teaching is a process involving (a) pinpointing the learner's performance levels, (b) delivering instruction using lesson plans and instructional strategies, and (c) recording data to determine progress and to make decisions about ongoing instruction. Teaching and learning are complex processes because each learner is unique and brings a dynamic and intricate patchwork of experiences, background, fears, anxieties, and dreams to the situation. Let's take a closer look at four learners and what they bring to the classroom.

Meet the Learners

 JANALYN

Janalyn is a 9-year-old girl from a low-income family. She attends an elementary school that qualifies for a free-lunch program. Janalyn works with a Title I paraeducator, Hakan, in reading. Hakan provides support for Janalyn's reading effort. When Janalyn finishes reading a sentence, she rarely recalls its meaning because her effort was focused on decoding the seemingly jumbled text. To Janalyn, a sentence like "The cow jumped over the moon" looks more like "Thecomjuwdeponerthewoon." Janalyn reverses letters and does not see separations between words.

Hakan understands that the first issue is to "unjumble" the text. He gently corrects errors and praises Janalyn for effort and success, then, inconspicuously, Hakan asks comprehension questions about the reading. "Can you believe that cow? What did he do?" asks Hakan. Janalyn is drawn back to the story. "He jumped!" she says. "Yes, Janalyn, he jumped. But what did he jump over?" asks Hakan. Janalyn looks back at the words on the page. Unsure, she pauses. Hakan starts, "He jumped over the m——. What did he jump over?" "The moon!" screams Janalyn. "Good. So what did he do again?" Hakan asks. "Tell me the whole thing." "He jumped over the moon," Janalyn responds. "Good!" Hakan pretends to be puzzled. "But wait a minute. Can a cow jump over the moon?" "No, Hakan," says Janalyn. "That's silly!"

SKYLOR

Skylor is a 14-year-old boy with autism spectrum disorder. Although Skylor is well accepted in his general education junior high classes, his academic skills are far below what would be expected for his age. He can recite his name, address, and phone number and can read some basic vocabulary words. However, he does not hold a pencil for more than a few seconds; instead, he flings it to the floor. Skylor seems to dislike holding things in his hands, especially if they produce a scratchy sensation, like a pencil on paper. His special education teacher and an occupational therapist developed a program to teach Skylor to hold a pencil with an adapted device. The device resembles a soft golf ball with a hole through which the pencil is inserted. They have asked the paraeducator, Robin, to work with Skylor in holding his adapted pencil in writing and arithmetic activities.

 KIMBERLY

Kimberly is a 10-year-old girl with fetal alcohol syndrome. Although Kimberly has no verbal language, she is learning to use a communication board with a synthesized voice. As Kimberly touches pictures on the board mounted on her wheelchair, the computer serves as her voice. The teacher, Shu-min, is teaching Kimberly to respond to questions by pressing keys labeled "yes" or "no." Shu-min has asked her paraeducator, Jeff, to assist Kimberly by guiding her to use the communication board.

 ANTONIO

Antonio is an 8-year-old boy who is learning to speak English. Antonio struggles to distinguish between the names of letters and their sounds. The same basic word list confronts him each day as if he had never seen it before. His parents, Mr. and Mrs. Ruiz, are new to the United States and understand Antonio's problems. They, too, struggle with a new language. A paraeducator in the classroom, Maria, assists Antonio in learning English. Maria introduces new words and shows how they represent objects or actions in Antonio's daily routine. She makes a list of new words each week and sends them to Mr. and Mrs. Ruiz.

The Paraeducator's Role in the Learning Process

Hakan, Robin, Jeff, and Maria play important roles in the learning process. Although planning instruction is the teacher's role, trained and well-supervised paraeducators may

1. deliver instruction to individual learners or small groups;
2. instruct learners in academic subjects using lesson plans and instructional strategies developed by teachers or other professional staff;
3. perform informal assessments of a learner's skills or behaviors;
4. record data on observations of a learner's skills or behaviors;
5. monitor learners performing independent practice of learned skills; and
6. use developmentally and age-appropriate instructional procedures.

The paraeducator's role varies depending on the age and characteristics of the learner, the type of school environment, and the job description developed by the district. Generally, given training and supervision, paraeducators perform specific tasks that include the following:

• *Academic tutoring and literacy development.* Some paraeducators spend much of their time working with individual learners or small groups. Like Hakan, many paraeducators work in Title I programs to assist children who have academic limitations and who are from low-income or economically disadvantaged families. They might read to learners; listen to learners read; and assist learners with math, language, writing, spelling, and other academic assignments. Paraeducators who assist in academic tutoring may demonstrate (i.e., model) correct responses, ask learners to imitate the model, await a response, praise and recognize correct imitation, or correct errors.

• *Activities of daily living.* Paraeducators who work with learners with more significant disabilities might assist in activities of daily living (such as health care, personal hygiene, dressing, laundry, etc.). These skills are usually taught in environments in which the skill is performed. For example, a paraeducator may assist in the teaching of hand-washing at a sink in the school restroom by demonstrating a specific task (such as turning on the hot and cold water), asking the learner to imitate the model, and praising or correcting the learner's response.

• *Inclusive classrooms.* Trained paraeducators play a major role in the inclusion process by helping learners in general education classrooms. In addition to playing important roles in academic instruction, paraeducators may introduce the learner to classmates and assist in teaching social skills.

• *Community and employment environments.* Some paraeducators assist individual learners who go to community sites for health care, therapy, or job training. For example, job coaches work with youth in an employment setting by teaching job tasks, "shadowing" the learner during performance of the task, gradually reducing support over time, and assisting in development of "natural supports" among other employees and supervisors.

• *Positive behavior support.* Some paraeducators work with learners who engage in problem behaviors. For these learners, the priority is developing appropriate social behavior using positive procedures. For example, a paraeducator receives instruction from a teacher or behavior specialist in how to carry out a positive behavior support plan for a learner who engages in aggressive behavior during math period. The paraeducator works with the learner by encouraging him to raise his hand to ask for help in math instead of ripping up an assignment.

What Works: Ways To Provide
Effective Instruction

Hofmeister and Lubke (1990) considered eight ways to provide effective instruction. These features are (a) assessment to pinpoint skill level, (b) active engagement, (c) instruction that targets the learner's skill level, (d) high rates of correct learner responses, (e) high rates of positive feedback from instructors, (f) immediate correction of errors, (g) maintenance of skills, and (h) generalization of skills. Regardless of the skill being taught or the type of instruction being used, these methods play a major role in increasing academic success.

Assessment to Pinpoint Skill Level

There are many different kinds of assessment. Informal assessments are nonstandardized tests of a learner's performance in an academic, social, or other skill area. The informal assessment process involves gathering data on a learner's skills, behaviors, and preferences (Snell & Brown, 2000). For example, a curriculum-based assessment (CBA) takes samples from curriculum areas to create an assessment instrument. A learner is then assessed to determine his or her instructional level in the curriculum. This information is useful in developing Individualized Education Program (IEP) goals and objectives and in determining progress over time. Paraeducators can administer informal assessment given adequate training and supervision. In most cases, certification or licensure is not required. Another kind of assessment, called "formal assessment," involves intelligence and achievement tests, which usually require certification or licensure (Snell & Brown, 2000).

Active Engagement

Learners acquire skills when they are actively engaged in the learning process. Active engagement means frequently writing, reading, responding to questions, or practicing new skills. For example, Kimberly, described in the Meet the Learners section, was actively engaged in using her communication board. Several times each minute, her paraeducator, Jeff, asked Kimberly to respond to yes and no questions. Also, Jeff showed Kimberly's classmates how to ask her questions. Kimberly frequently practiced the skills that she would use in her natural environment. Paraeducators actively engage learners by asking them frequent questions, directing them to engage in tasks, and recognizing their responses. When appropriate, paraeducators can encourage learners to communicate with each other.

Instruction That Targets the Learner's Skill Level

A teacher carefully selects instructional material based on the learner's current skill level. Although the teacher's role is to select instructional material, paraeducators can assist in three ways:

1. *Check for "prerequisite skills" (i.e., those taught in earlier lessons).* Prior to starting a lesson involving new material, ask individual learners to perform tasks or answer questions taught in previous lessons. If the learner cannot perform the task or answers incorrectly, correct the error and report the finding to the supervising teacher. This might mean the learner is not prepared to start a new lesson.

2. *Observe the learner's performance, and pinpoint it in the curriculum.* That is, identify exactly where the learner's skills fall in the sequence of skills taught by a curriculum. Teachers are responsible for identifying the level of instruction for learners, but paraeducators can often pinpoint exactly where a child is performing. For example, the teacher knows that Aurelio is working on 2-digit subtraction with regrouping, but his paraeducator, Vanessa, has observed that Aurelio does not borrow "10" when he tries to subtract. Vanessa can inform the teacher that Aurelio needs more work on how to borrow in subtraction.

3. *Ask learners to perform tasks or answer questions that are equal to or slightly higher than their current skill level.* If a learner appears bored or off task, the learner's instructional level may be set slightly higher. If the learner appears frustrated, the instructional level should be set slightly lower. In either case, report the findings to the teacher.

High Rates of Correct Responses

Learners should respond frequently to provide evidence that they are learning. Effective instructors (i.e., teachers or trained and well-supervised paraeducators) call on learners frequently to answer questions or to respond during a lesson. Lessons should combine learned material with new material in such a way that the learner responds correctly to 80% to 90% of opportunities (Hofmeister & Lubke, 1990). At these levels, learners can be frequently recognized for their success and remain motivated to receive additional instruction. The remaining 10% to 20% of responses are errors to be corrected by the instructor. When teachers develop lesson plans, questions or tasks must be carefully crafted to match the learner's performance level. If an instructor "overshoots" a learner's level by including a complex item that results in an incorrect answer, he or she should follow it with a simpler item.

High Rates of Positive Feedback

Many children have long histories of academic failure and helplessness. They feel anxious and vulnerable when learning a new skill because they fear another failure. Effective instructors recognize each small success for learners. Initially, every correct response should be followed by a statement of praise or recognition (Morgan, Forbush, & Avis, 2001). As a skill becomes mastered, effective instructors gradually reduce praise and recognition.

Immediate Correction of Errors

A learner's errors should not go uncorrected. Imagine the frustration if Antonio, the 8-year-old boy struggling to learn English, continued to practice errors, only to find out much later that they were incorrect. Uncorrected errors can result in incorrect habits and even hinder learning of new skills. Correction should be immediate and delivered in a neutral way using a regular voice tone. Avoid appearing frustrated with the learner. Delayed correction may be ineffective because, to the learner, the feedback is unrelated to the original error.

Maintenance of Skills

Unless skills are frequently practiced, they disappear; therefore, learners must frequently practice skills to maintain them. Even mastered skills can disappear without practice. To the effective instructor, this means scheduling frequent practice opportunities as skills are being learned. In addition, it means arranging frequent checks, even after skills have been mastered.

Generalization of Skills

Learners rarely perform skills only with the original instructor or only in one location. Learners usually perform skills in situations involving several different people, places, and things. That is, skills must "generalize," or transfer, to new situations. To the effective instructor, this means checking new skills with a different person, or in a different place, or with new materials.

Key Steps in Delivering Instruction

Instruction can be delivered to individual learners or to groups. Trained paraeducators may apply the following steps when working under the supervision of a teacher (paraeducators may apply these steps only with training and when working under the supervision of a teacher): (a) getting the learner's attention; (b) delivering information in short, specific quantities; (c) calling for a response; (d) waiting for a response; (e) affirming correct responses; and (f) correcting all errors (Morgan et al., 2001).

◆ *Step 1: Get the learner's attention.* Instructors should not begin presenting information unless they have the learner's attention. This is especially critical if working with learners who have severe disabilities or who have problems sustaining attention.

 1. Use the learner's name *before* presenting information.

    Incorrect: "Come on, look up here. Hey, up here, Marco."
    Correct: "Marco, look at me."

 2. Obtain eye contact from the learner to establish attention.

◆ *Step 2: Deliver new information in small quantities.* Provide a small amount of new information to the learner in a lesson; the amount of new information depends on the learner. If the learner remains engaged and responds correctly to new information, the amount is probably appropriate and therefore may be increased slightly. Ask the supervising teacher for advice. Instructors present information by telling, showing, or using combinations of telling and showing. Use communication systems that are familiar. For example,

> Marco, look at me. Thanks! Watch me. First, I'm going to hold the lace like this. Then, I'll put the lace through the hole like this. Marco, it's your turn. Hold the lace.

◆ *Step 3: Call for a response.* After presenting information, it is the learner's turn. Make sure learners understand when it is their turn to respond.

◆ *Step 4: Wait for a response.* For most learners, pause at least 3 to 5 seconds. It is often helpful to count silently to yourself. Do not interrupt the count by responding for the learner. If you do, you may be denying the child a valuable learning opportunity. If the learner does not respond, call again for a response.

◆ *Step 5: Affirm correct responses.* Praise and describe the correct response and then move immediately to the next learning task or next trial.

◆ *Step 6: Correct all errors.* Again, always correct an error. Do not allow errors to go uncorrected.

Three different kinds of learner's errors and ways to correct them follow:

• *A learner's error may suggest inattention to the key information.* Many times learners lose track of relevant information or have difficulty distinguishing relevant from irrelevant information. Instructors should break a problem down into smaller steps for the learner. One way is to ask a "leading question." Leading questions prompt the learner to consider the sequence of events (e.g., What happened first? What comes next?) or focus on relevant material (e.g., Where do you write the number you are carrying?). By asking leading questions, the instructor can direct a learner to the correct answer by emphasizing the relevant aspects of the problem. Instructors can use this procedure when a learner is having difficulty with math problems, reading comprehension, vocational tasks, or other activities composed of multiple steps. For example,

Leading Question	Response
What is the first thing you do when you multiply 34 by 6?	Multiply 4 times 6.
That's right, and what is 4 times 6?	24.
Twenty-four is right. And so what do you write down?	4, carry the 2…

• *A learner's error may suggest that he or she started the task but became confused.* In this case, the learner recalled the initial part of a task but encountered something that he or she did not anticipate. To correct the error, the instructor should restate the learner's initial response, then ask "What happens next?" or "Tell me more." For example,

OK, you say the boy in the story wanted to ride the horse. That's right. Now, tell me what happened when he tried to get on the horse.

If the learner is still unable to recall the information, break the task into smaller parts. For example,

I don't remember what happened when he tried to get on the horse. When he walked up to the horse, what did the horse do?

If the learner still cannot recall, provide the information to the learner.

3. *A learner's error may suggest that she or he is missing important facts.* If a learner is missing important facts that are necessary to answer a problem correctly or to perform a task, the instructor must provide the information to the learner. If the learner is a part of a group, announce the information to the whole group so the learner is not singled out. Return to the learner at a later time to review the information. For example, Jarron, a high-school-age learner, is a member of a transition work crew learning to mow lawns. Today, he cannot start the lawn mower. His paraeducator approaches and checks the mower, then addresses the entire crew. "Hey, everybody," she says, "Before we can start a mower, we check the height adjustments, the safety start switch, the position of the choke, and what else?" (One crewmember says "Gas tank.") "That's right," she says, "Check

the gas tank. This gas tank is empty. What do we do?" (Another crew-member responds.) "Yes, that's right," she says, "We need to put gas in the tank."

Physical Prompting

Learners sometimes need physical prompting as temporary help in per-forming motor activities, such as basic self-help skills (e.g., buttoning, zipping, washing hands). After they have received training and direction from the supervising teacher, paraeducators may use physical prompting with young learners or with those who have significant disabilities. Physi-cal prompting can be used to present information or to correct errors. Here are two guidelines:

1. Use the least amount of physical prompting necessary for the learner to correct the error. (The learner might become overly dependent on the assistance if an instructor uses too much assis-tance for too long.)
2. Before using physical prompts, determine whether the learner is comfortable being touched. (Some learners react negatively to physical touch, or a learner's parents or guardians might prefer no touching. Check with the supervising teacher.)

When correcting errors using physical prompting, the goal is for the learner to perform the task with the least assistance. Before using physi-cal prompting, tell the learner what is required. Use the least prompting necessary to obtain a correct response, and use a sequence of actions (see Figure 3.1).

Excessive Prompting and "Taking Over"

Sometimes paraeducators believe that staying near a learner is part of their job and that the best way to help is to take over tasks for learners. These beliefs are false. In fact, staying close to the learner and taking over might be harmful, for several reasons (Giangreco, Edelman, Luiselli, & MacFarland, 1997). Staying close and taking over

1. separates learners from classmates,
2. produces dependence on adults,

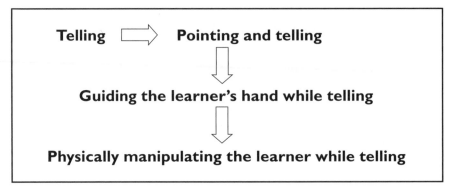

Figure 3.1. A sequence of actions in physical prompting.

3. reduces communication between learners and peers, and
4. restricts participation in instructional activities.

Effective instructors do just enough to allow learners to learn but not so much to deny them learning opportunities. In some situations, it is difficult to tell the difference between what is enough and what is too much. When in doubt, talk to the supervising teacher.

The Paraeducator's Role in the Lesson Plan

With adequate training and supervision, paraeducators may use lesson plans to deliver instruction. Lesson plans are specific, daily instructional activities designed by teachers (Hofmeister & Lubke, 1990) that usually include the following key components: (a) prelesson review (i.e., a brief assessment of previously learned skills); (b) model or demonstration (i.e., showing or telling the learner what to do); (c) guided practice (i.e., guiding the learner in practicing the response); (d) independent practice (i.e., watching the learner perform the response without assistance); and (e) data collection (i.e., recording data on the learner's performance). The paraeducator's responsibilities are to follow the plan, ask questions for clarification, and seek guidance from the supervising teacher to better deliver instruction.

The Paraeducator's Role in Instructional Settings, Management, and Groupings

Instruction is most effective if it takes place in the setting where the skill will be used. For example, the best place to teach bus safety skills is in and around a school bus. However, because of limitations in schedules or resources, instruction must sometimes occur in other settings. For example, in a classroom setting, to simulate shopping at a supermarket, the teacher may cut out newspaper ads with product prices and have learners compute the costs of a shopping trip.

Paraeducators work with individual learners and small groups. In both cases, management of instruction is important (see guidelines in Figure 3.2).

Presession Management Steps:

1. Prepare and organize the instructional materials.
2. Keep materials within your reach, not the learner's reach.
3. Greet the learners and provide praise for getting ready and having their materials (pencils, paper, etc.) prepared.

Session Management Steps:

1. State the goal of instruction and the rationale for teaching the specific skill.
2. Particularly when working with groups, announce a few basic rules and expectations. Describe rules for how the learners and instructor will take turns, how learners should get the instructor's attention, and how learners should respond when addressed.
3. Establish positive consequences for following rules. Praise compliance with rules.
4. Seat the distractible or more active learners nearest you.
5. Increase voice volume slightly above conversational level. Use your voice tone to emphasize key points in the lesson.
6. Avoid questions from learners that detract from instruction; instead, politely tell the learner that you will answer the question later. Avoid "going off on a tangent."
7. Position yourself so that learners can see your face and the instructional materials. Do not turn your back to learners or cover your mouth, particularly when working with learners who have hearing impairments.

Figure 3.2. Management of instruction with individual learners or groups.

The Paraeducator's Role with Learners

Janalyn is a 9-year-old girl, Skylor is a 14-year-old boy, Kimberly is a 10-year-old girl, and Antonio is an 8-year-old boy. Like all children, they are unique in their learning styles and preferences. The paraeducator can help to identify the learning style of each learner; more than any team member, the paraeducator is in a strategic position to gather information on how learners learn. The following are questions paraeducators can ask themselves about individual learning styles:

1. What is the learner's most effective and reliable modality (i.e., method of learning)—visual, auditory, or touch?
2. Can modalities (e.g., visual and auditory modalities) be combined to present new information to the learner? For example, can you tell *and* show a learner how to do a task and get better performance than just telling or showing alone? For some learners, combining modalities works very well. For others, this may be confusing or overwhelming.
3. How much new information can the learner manage at a time? To maintain high rates of correct responses, amount of new information should be limited. However, as the learner performs well on smaller amounts, more material can be added. Previously learned material should be frequently reviewed.
4. What positive reinforcers can follow correct responses to enhance learning? Are there "natural" reinforcers to be used (i.e., ones that result from completing the task itself, such as eating a sandwich after making it)?
5. What environments are best for the individual learner (e.g., quiet ones without distractions, environments in which actual skills will be used)?

Answers to these questions will assist the paraeducator and teacher in tailoring the learning experience to the needs and preferences of the individual learner. The paraeducator and teacher may want to create an "individual profile" describing the learning style of each learner.

Summary

This chapter examines the paraeducator's role in the instructional process. Although paraeducators are becoming more integral parts of classroom instruction, their instructional roles must remain distinct and separate from the roles of the teacher. Paraeducators can do much, however, to strengthen the instructional process. Paraeducators should dedicate their efforts to supporting teachers in creating and maintaining the best possible learning environment for all learners. This commitment requires examining the features that make instruction effective and practicing the key components of effective instruction.

ACTIVITIES

1. An effective instructor asks learners frequent questions and gets several responses per minute. Even within the context of routine tasks, effective instructors can generate questions. For example, while walking with a learner to the general education class, an effective instructor can ask questions about shapes of bricks in the wall, signs on the wall, colors of coats on racks, numbers on classroom doors, school rules about walking in hallways, spellings of names of people encountered in the hall, and so forth. Select a routine task, describe the location of the task, and write a list of five questions that you could use to engage a learner during this task.

2. The next time you work with learners, count the frequency of your "good job" statements. Also, count your specific praise statements (e.g., "Nice work—you tied both shoes!" "Excellent work on your math today—90% correct!"). Which statements are higher in frequency? Specific praise statements are advantageous over "good job" statements because they inform the learner of the precise action being recognized. Resolve to finish the statement: "Good job." That is, when you catch yourself saying "good job," at least finish the statement by telling the learner, for example, "Good job for finishing your math assignment." If you are working with your teacher or another paraeducator, ask him or her to assist you in finishing "good job" statements.

3. Interview three teachers. Ask each of them "What makes instruction effective?" Write notes on their answers and then compare the three sets of responses. What similarities and differences were found?

4. Read the case study that follows and answer the questions, either individually or in a group-discussion activity.

TAMIKA

Tamika was a paraeducator working at Lincoln High School. She was supervised by Mrs. Charles, the resource teacher, but she often accompanied learners to general education classes. During fourth period she worked with Rashan in his 10th-grade literature class. Rashan was a poor reader who expressed strong dislike for his literature class and for Tamika. Mrs. Charles developed lesson plans adapting reading activities to Rashan's instructional level. Tamika's job was to carry out the lessons in the literature class. After days of painstaking trials with Rashan, Mrs. Charles and Tamika considered a different approach. Somehow, they needed to make reading a relevant and useful skill for Rashan. Mrs. Charles suggested that Tamika ask Rashan questions about his interests. She reasoned that she and Tamika could design reading instruction around Rashan's favorite topics. Rashan refused to respond to the questions. Mrs. Charles and Tamika brainstormed other ideas. They wrote partial sentences with no endings, such as "If I could go anywhere right now, I would go _____." Rashan immediately responded to these sentences by describing his interest in contemporary music, particularly hip-hop, soul, and blues. Mrs. Charles and Tamika researched musicians, lyrics, songs, and pop culture. They developed lesson plans based on Rashan's favorite artists. At first, Rashan objected and pointed out errors in his teacher's information. Mrs. Charles saw her error as an opportunity. "Okay, Rashan, I don't know who Robert Johnson was. So help me out. Where can I find out about him?" Rashan was now a partner in developing his lesson plans. He and Tamika found books at the library. Tamika purchased magazines on pop music for Rashan to read. They found connections between literature class topics and music. Rashan slowly began interacting with the entire class. Reading, although still frustrating for Rashan, became tolerable. What else could Mrs. Charles and Tamika have done to develop a partnership with Rashan? From your own experience, in what ways can you enlist the support of learners?

Discussion Questions

1. After correcting an error, why is retesting necessary?

2. How can you adapt the error-correction procedures for learners who have no verbal language or for learners who are learning English as a second language?

3. How do you know when you are prompting excessively? How do you gauge the right amount of prompting?

References

Giangreco, M. F., Edelman, S. W., Luiselli, T. E., & MacFarland, S. Z. C. (1997). Helping or hovering? Effects of instructional assistant proximity on students with disabilities. *Exceptional Children, 64*(1), 7–18.

Hofmeister, A., & Lubke, M. (1990). *Research into practice: Implementing effective strategies.* Boston: Allyn & Bacon.

Morgan, R. L., Forbush, D. E., & Avis, D. (2001). *Enhancing skills of paraeducators: A video-assisted program* (2nd ed.). Logan: Utah State University.

Snell, M. E., & Brown, F. (2000). *Instruction of students with severe disabilities* (5th ed.). Upper Saddle River, NJ: Merrill.

Promoting Positive Behavior: What Works and What Doesn't

4

Marilyn Likins and Debra Andrews

Behavior is a critical part of any educational setting involving children. Teachers and staff members spend an inordinate amount of time dealing with inappropriate behavior, and behavior problems have been cited as a major cause of educators' leaving the classroom and finding alternative careers (U.S. Office of Special Edu. Programs Technical Assistance Center on Positive Behavioral Interventions and Support, 1999). As key members of instructional teams, paraeducators are well aware of the behavior and discipline challenges that can be found in today's classrooms. Not only are they hired to provide instructional services and effectively manage the learning environment, but also they are frequently asked to supervise learners during recess, in the halls, before and after school, at lunch, or while riding the bus to and from school. Paraeducators are therefore often the "first on the scene" when inappropriate behaviors occur. For this reason, promoting positive behaviors and managing inappropriate ones are critical skill targets for most paraeducators. Additionally, it is imperative to adhere to ethical and professional responsibilities when working with students who have behavioral challenges. These responsibilities include treating learners with dignity and respect when implementing behavior management strategies, exercising self-restraint when engaged in emotional situations, and respecting the learner's privacy.

Are learner behaviors becoming more difficult to handle or more frequent? Conflicting research states that learner misbehaviors may or may not be more intense or more prevalent in the classrooms today. Educators must become more efficient and effective at being behavior managers rather than focusing solely on learners' behaviors. When they are hired, many paraeducators may ask, "What is my role when it comes to managing problem behaviors?" Commonly articulated roles for paraeducators include (a) using proactive management strategies to engage learners and (b) supporting the supervisor's behavior management plan. The purpose of this chapter is to help paraeducators and their supervisors understand how supporting a positive learning environment translates into effective management practices in their educational setting.

Learning Objectives

After reading this chapter, paraeducators should be able to do the following:

1. Define *behavior* and discuss the relationship between the behavior and events that occur in the environment
2. Describe what we know about behavior
3. Describe the ABCs of behavior
4. Discuss the three basic functions that behavior typically serves
5. Discuss reasons why learners misbehave and possible solutions
6. Discuss "how" and "why" we measure behavior
7. Describe proactive management strategies for increasing behaviors
8. Describe proactive strategies for increasing compliance
9. Discuss the steps of a precision command
10. Define reinforcement and discuss types of reinforcement
11. Describe "planned ignoring" and "selective attention" and when to use such strategies

Key Terms and Definitions

The following key terms and definitions will be used throughout this chapter.

Antecedent. Events that predictably precede and trigger problem behavior (e.g., task demands, instruction, adult requests)

Behavior management. The implementation of positive and reductive behavior-based strategies to shape and direct student behavior and ensure student success—both academically and behaviorally

Consequence. Events that occur following or as a result of the behavior

Duration of a behavior. A record of the exact starting and ending time of a behavior and the length of time the behavior occurred

Extinction. Withholding reinforcement for a behavior that was previously reinforced for the purpose of reducing the occurrence of that behavior

Fading. Gradually decreasing over time cues, prompts, reminders, and reinforcers that control a specific behavior

Frequency count. A record of the number of times a specific behavior occurs within a time period

Functional behavioral assessment. A process that includes using a variety of techniques and strategies to discover the causes of problem behavior and to identify interventions that will address those problem behaviors (functional behavioral assessment looks beyond the obvious dimensions of a behavior and focuses instead on identifying other related factors that set off, prolong, or stop the behavior)

Modeling. Demonstrating a new behavior so that a learner might acquire the skill by observing it

Negative reinforcement. Removing or reducing the intensity of an environmental condition (usually something unpleasant) that increases a behavior's rate of occurrence

Positive behavior supports (PBS). The application of positive behavioral interventions and systems to achieve socially important behavior change in students

Positive reinforcement. Providing a consequence following a behavior that increases the behavior's rate of occurrence

Precision command (or precision request). A precise verbal statement made by staff members to enhance learner compliance

Prompting. The use of verbal, physical, and visual cues to encourage a particular response

Punishment. A consequence that follows behavior and decreases the behavior's future rate of occurrence

Rate. The ratio of the number of times a behavior occurs within a specific time period *and* the length of the time period

Replacement behavior. Behaviors taught to the learner that serve the same function as the inappropriate behaviors

Shaping. Systematically reinforcing a learner's approximations of the desired behavior until the learner can demonstrate the behavior successfully over time

Problem Behavior: A Case Example

Problem behaviors are day-to-day occurrences in our schools. Recognizing that you can be a part of the problem or part of the solution is the first step in knowing what to do. Consider the following scenario.

 PAT

Pat, a paraeducator, is supervising a classroom of ninth-grade learners while the teacher leaves to make a quick call. The bell rings. The learners file into their seats and begin to slowly get out the assigned work. Pat notices that Charlene comes in excited and noisy. When she reaches her desk, she drops her backpack on the floor with a loud thud and then sits turned backward in her seat while continuing to talk to her peers. Pat says, "Charlene, get your work out and get started, okay?" Charlene takes several seconds to finish her conversation and then turns around in her seat, getting out her books and papers, and begins her assignment.

David, on the other hand, comes in quietly and sits at a desk in the back of the classroom. Immediately he lays his head on his desk and covers his face with his arms. Pat repeats the same type of request for David, "Hey David, it's time to work on your assignment, okay? Don't you want to get it finished? Won't you need your book? Where is your book? Where is your paper? Did you bring a pencil?" David looks up at Pat, says, "@*&*^# you! I hate this stupid class!" He knocks the desk over and storms out of the classroom. Immediately overwhelmed with frustration and anger, Pat follows David into the hallway and yells at him to come back. "David, you did NOT have permission to leave the classroom! You'd better come back!" David continues down the hall. Pat returns to the classroom, where the learners are laughing and talking loudly. It takes Pat another 7 to 8 minutes to get the learners back on task.

What happened? What did Pat do to deserve this kind of treatment? If David was having a bad day, why couldn't he just tell her? What should Pat have done instead?

The most common response to this kind of situation is anger and frustration—angry adults and angry kids. Typically in this type of situation the adult does not take the time or make the effort to try to figure out where the problem began and if he or she actually contributed to the outburst. However, without that kind of analysis we can ensure that similar problems will happen again, and again, and again…. So, what do we do? If paraeducators are likely to be in situations where they will have to effectively deal with problem behaviors, they must first understand behavior and why it occurs. In addition, paraeducators must have knowledge about effective interventions for managing difficult behaviors. Let's get started.

Many instructors, teachers, and paraeducators make common discipline mistakes, including engaging in verbal battles, yelling, warning learners with no follow-through, reprimanding learners in front of their peers, and using sarcasm or force. Rather than decreasing the problem behavior, such discipline mistakes frequently lead to an escalation of the problem behavior.

Typical problem behavior found in the majority of classrooms today falls into two categories: inconsequential and consequential. Latham (2000) defined "inconsequential" behavior as those problem behaviors that are annoying and frustrating. They include talkouts, out of seat, complaining, tattling, and so forth. On the other hand, "consequential" inappropriate behavior is behavior that hurts, damages, or destroys, such as physical aggression, destruction of property, sustained disruption of the learning environment, and so forth. A good classroom behavior management plan or schoolwide plan effectively addresses both of these types of behavior.

As a paraeducator, it is your role to become familiar with your supervisor's management plan or schoolwide plan and assist in implementing effective management strategies on a day-to-day basis. How does this happen? It happens through ongoing discussions, in-service training, and on-the-job coaching and feedback. Effective management practices work regardless of who is implementing them. Consequently, if all instructional team members are trained to use the same proactive strategies to engage learners in the task at hand, learners' behavior will change. The key is consistency across staff members.

As you work with learners and staff members, remember, "The only person's behavior you can control is your own." With this in mind, we will explore the basic principles of behavior and several proactive management strategies over which you have total control. For example, to increase appropriate behaviors, it is critical to maintain a high rate of positive consequences by "catching learners being good." Learners should be taught classroom rules as well as procedures and expectations at the beginning of the school year; then it is everyone's job to look for learners who are following those rules and working cooperatively and to acknowledge their behavior with positive gestures (e.g., head nod, wink, pat on the back) or praise statements. Behaviors increase with reinforcement, so be sure you focus attention on the behaviors you want to improve (e.g., staying in seat, working on the assigned task, following directions).

When inconsequential behaviors occur, strategies such as planned ignoring paired with frequent use of proximity praise keep other learners on task and engaged. Using planned ignoring or extinction is simple. When misbehavior occurs, break eye contact, turn and walk away from the misbehaving learner, and purposely continue with another activity. It is vital that you do not attend to, look at, or acknowledge the learner's behavior in any way. Be aware that when you withhold your attention, the behavior may escalate or get worse before it gets better. Resist the urge to give in. Keep yourself occupied by praising others nearby who exhibit the behavior you want (i.e., proximity praise) and do not forget to praise the target learner when he or she exhibits the appropriate behavior.

Occasionally learners will do things that cannot be ignored because they interfere with learning, pose a danger to themselves or others, or seriously violate classroom or school rules. When consequential behavior occurs, it is important to intervene as soon as you observe the problem behavior; it will typically escalate and be harder to correct at a later point.

What Is Behavior?

To learn about behavior, it is important to first define *behavior*. Webster (Mish, 1998, p.103) defines *behavior* as "a way of behaving or conducting onself." For the purposes of investigation, something a little more specific and descriptive is needed. The following is a basis from which we can go forward with our study of human behavior.

Behavior is any action that can be seen (observed) *and* can be counted (measured) (Baer, Wolf, & Risley, 1968). This is an important concept to understand. Many times when we describe what we think of as *behavior,* we make some minor mistakes. The common mistakes are (a) making assumptions about how someone *feels* or what he or she *thinks,* and (b) using descriptions for responses that we cannot see or count. Let's look at some examples:

1. Juan was frustrated about his work.
   a. What is the assumption?
   The assumption is that he is feeling frustrated.
   b. What can or cannot be seen or counted?
   "Frustration" cannot be seen or counted.
   c. What is a better way to describe the behavior? (What does his behavior look and sound like?)
   Juan is not completing his work and he is ripping the papers by frequent erasing. He is talking loudly and saying things such as "I can't do this!" or "Nobody will help me and I don't know how to do this assignment!"

2. Melissa was angry when she didn't get to be the class representative for Learner Council.
   a. What is the assumption?
   The assumption is that she is feeling angry.
   b. What can or cannot be seen or counted?
   "Anger" is assumed when we see the display of behaviors that we associate with anger; however, it cannot be counted.
   c. What is a better way to describe the behavior?
   When she was not elected to the Learner Council, Melissa stamped her foot, folded her arms, made faces, began to cry, and yelled, "That's not fair!"

Now complete this one on your own.

3. Yuriko is lazy and unmotivated in this classroom.
   a. What is the assumption?
   b. What can or cannot be seen or counted?
   c. What might be a better way to describe the behavior?

Still finding it difficult? Don't worry. We'll talk more about describing behavior later on. Just remember…a behavior is an event that can be seen *and* counted.

What Do We Know About Behavior?

Many years of research have taught us some important lessons about behavior. In this section, we will discuss the concepts and ideas concerning behavior that have been proven time and time again through observation and investigation.

Almost All Behavior Is Learned

When you visualize tiny newborn babies, you realize that they don't have many behaviors in their repertoires. Initially, infants sleep, eat, eliminate, and cry. Within a matter or hours after birth, a baby learns that "crying" will quickly bring food, cuddling, and a diaper change. Within months, other behaviors are learned, and the baby uses these behaviors to get what he or she wants or needs. The child's behavioral repertoire continues to grow larger and larger.

Once we realize that a child develops these behaviors early and continues to use the same actions as he or she gets older, we can see how skilled a child can become at using those behaviors that bring success. It is unfortunate that many times children will use inappropriate behaviors to get their wants and needs met. If using the inappropriate behaviors has proven successful, a child will use those same behaviors over and over again to continue to get what he or she wants.

Throughout our lifetimes, we as humans continue to learn and use behaviors that will assist us in obtaining what we need or desire. We continue to use those behaviors that give us success. We cease to use behaviors that are unproductive or inefficient. For the most part, we do this without thinking too much about it. Behavior is something that we engage in without much forethought or planning. When a child throws a tantrum in the grocery store because he or she wants a toy, it is probably because that same behavior resulted in success once or twice before. The child did not likely plan and predict what would happen at the store. Human behavior also communicates what we might be thinking or feeling. Remember, when a behavior occurs, don't make assumptions about the emotion behind it—report only what is observed.

All Behavior Is Communication

Let's get back to our infant. It is apparent that infants experience emotions at a very early age. Infants laugh, cry, and show signs of fear and anger. Unfortunately, language does not develop at the same rate as a child's emotions or feelings. Have you ever heard an infant tell you that she is experiencing a great deal of frustration and anger because she cannot walk to the refrigerator to get a snack? Not likely. When a child (or anyone) does not have the capacity to verbalize or otherwise tell someone how he or she is feeling, behavior often serves as the most natural form of communication. This is also true of older children, adolescents, adults, and persons with disabilities who have communication difficulties. Understanding what a behavior is communicating is critical in determining why that behavior is occurring and how it might be changed (Carr & Durand, 1985).

More often than not, with the use of observation and experience, we can predict what a child is attempting to say through his or her behavior. Here are some sample behaviors that are communicating some type of need.

Behavior	Possible Reason
Yawning	Fatigue
Crying	Discomfort (hungry, fatigued, wet, etc.)

All Behavior Serves a Function and Purpose

Even the most simple and basic behaviors serve a function for an individual. Blinking one's eyes keeps them moist and clean. Closing the windows keeps the cold air and rain out of a home. Grabbing a toy and running results in a child's being chased by a peer. Typically, we engage in behaviors that will result in getting something we need or want or will satisfy some type of physical or emotional need. When examining a behavior, ask "What is this individual gaining from this behavior?" Remember, appearances can be deceiving. The learner may appear to get nothing or to receive only negative consequences from the behavior and yet persist in doing it. What may appear to be a negative consequence, however, may in fact be rewarding to the learner. To effectively analyze the functions of a particular behavior, we must remember that what may be punishing to one learner may be reinforcing to another, and vice versa.

Behavior Is 100%—100% of the Time

Human beings are constantly behaving. There is not a time, place, or situation when behavior is not occurring. Commonly, we attempt to "get rid of" the behaviors that we do not like or that cause problems for the learner, the instructors, or others in the class. When you punish these behaviors, you will probably see a change in the behavior right away. Unfortunately, this is a temporary solution to the problem. When using punishment to stop a behavior, the learner may indeed stop using that behavior for the moment but will likely return to that behavior or adopt another behavior to get the desired result. Keep in mind that when you take something away, it is best to add something in its place. If you "get rid of" a behavior, you must replace it with a more appropriate, acceptable, and efficient behavior that will get the learner what he or she desires.

For example, Michael frequently interrupts discussions in class. The team has decided to work on decreasing his "talking out" in the class discussions. They should also consider working on "quiet hand-raising" or "waiting to be called on by the instructor" before making a comment.

In another example, McKenzie is physically aggressive with her peers. She hits them when they do not give her the toy that she wants. The team has decided to punish her hitting behavior by requiring her to take a seat away from the play area when she hits. They will *also* work on increasing her skills to communicate her desire by saying "May I have a turn with that toy?" and on how to accept a "no" response from the peer. They will teach her to go to another area or look for another toy if the peer says no.

The ABCs of Behavior

A clear understanding of the context in which behaviors are displayed is required for effectively addressing the unique needs of learners. Identifying the events, situations, or people who may trigger or support inappropriate behavior and then doing something about it proactively increases the likelihood of positive outcomes (O'Neill, Horner, Albin, Sprague, Storey, & Newton, 1997).

To understand behavior, we must first look at the relationship between the behavior and events that occur in the environment. We look for an observable pattern or relationship between a behavior and what occurs immediately before and after the behavior. The events that precede the behavior are referred to as the *antecedents*. The events that follow the behavior are referred to as the *consequences* (Skinner, 1953).

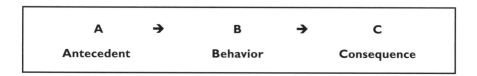

Antecedents can include

1. time of day;
2. a certain classroom or location;
3. the absence or presence of particular people;
4. specific statements, requests, or tasks; and
5. boredom or lack of stimulation.

Antecedents can include a combination of one or more of these conditions as well as other factors that are not listed. Consequences, the events or conditions that occur directly after a behavior, can be positive or negative. Although many things may occur following a behavior, consequences directly result from or are related to the behavior. Consequences may include

1. getting out of a task or situation,
2. having access to an item or object,
3. having access to a person or place,
4. getting attention from adults or peers,
5. receiving restrictions or extra work, and
6. being ignored by adults or peers.

Consequences may be either positive or negative. For many of us, a positive consequence for the behavior "going to work" is receiving a paycheck at the end of the month. A positive consequence of the behavior "studying for an exam" is getting a passing grade. Negative consequences include being criticized by the instructor for giving an incorrect answer in class or being ignored by peers after teasing them in the lunchroom. *Caution*: Negative consequences may result in a behavior happening more often. Remember, appearances can be deceiving—what might look like a negative consequence might actually act as a reinforcer for an individual. For example, Jonah likes to play the class clown by joking and making funny comments and gestures during instruction. The instructor stops the lesson and reprimands Jonah for his behavior. Over the next few days, the instructor notices an increase rather than a decrease in Jonah's disruptive behavior. After talking with colleagues, the instructor realizes that the reprimands actually served to give Jonah her undivided attention as well as that of all the others in the classroom. What initially appeared to be a punishment was actually reinforcing his disruptive behavior.

The key to understanding a learner's behavior is to observe it over time and begin to see patterns and relationships between behavior and those events or conditions that occur just prior to or immediately following the behavior. The only way to know for sure if an event or condition acts as a positive or negative consequence is to observe its effect on the behavior. If the behavior increases, it is a positive or motivating consequence. Likewise, if the behavior decreases, it is likely perceived by the learner as a negative consequence or punisher.

Functions of Behavior

As mentioned before, all behavior serves a function or purpose. To understand the basic ideas behind these functions, the majority of them can be categorized into the following three main areas (O'Neill et al., 1997; Skinner, 1953):

1. Gaining attention or accessing a desired object, activity, or individual
2. Escaping or avoiding a task, activity, or individual
3. Accessing sensory stimulation

Gaining Attention or Access

Gaining attention is a common reason for learners to demonstrate specific behaviors, whether that attention is from peers, instructors, or other adults. Many gain attention by using behaviors that are appropriate and socially acceptable, such as raising a hand to ask a question or to make a comment in class. Others use inappropriate behaviors to gain attention, such as making comments in class that are unsuitable or disruptive. The attention gained may be considered positive or negative; the perception of the learner determines the type of attention that is received. Typically, a learner who is being reprimanded for misbehavior will perceive the attention as negative. Keep in mind, however, that a learner who is actively *seeking* attention when there is little or none available (the instructor is ignoring or paying attention to others) is easily reinforced. The type of attention he or she receives is irrelevant or less important than receiving *any* attention. Negative attention is more reinforcing than no attention at all. Attention seeking can be an attempt to communicate needs and desires or an attempt to solicit positive reinforcement using a learned pattern of behavior resulting in a means to access people, objects, or events.

Instructor attention (positive reinforcement) is usually inconsistently given. An instructor might attend to a learner's behavior some times and ignore that same behavior at other times. This inconsistent pattern of giving attention reinforces or strengthens the use of inappropriate behavior. An example of "gaining access to objects, activities, or individuals" is a child who wants to play with a group of learners playing Four Square at recess and who interrupts the game by grabbing the ball. Asking to be included in the game is a more appropriate way of gaining access to the activity.

Means of Escape or Avoidance (Negative Reinforcement)

Behavior may also provide a learner with a way to escape or avoid an unpleasant situation or task. For example, Bubba does not like long-division problems; he finds them frustrating and difficult to solve. As the teacher asks learners to solve problems at the board, Bubba disrupts the class by talking out, making noises, teasing other learners, and throwing papers. After giving him numerous verbal warnings, the teacher sends Bubba out of the class and to the administrator's office, and so Bubba successfully avoids having to demonstrate his inability to do the math problems in front of his peers. Bubba might feel that getting in trouble is more acceptable than being perceived as "dumb" by his peers and the teacher. Escape or avoidance can be

1. an attempt to escape or avoid something external (external stimuli), for example, adult or peer attention, a difficult task, change in routine, a specific setting, some type of physical or environmental discomfort, or social embarrassment; or
2. an attempt to escape or avoid something internal (internal stimuli), for example, pain, hunger, and fatigue.

Sensory Feedback or Stimulation (Automatic Reinforcement)

Numerous behaviors may gain sensory stimulation, feedback, or both. For example, a learner who uses illegal substances gains automatic sensory stimulation. He receives reinforcement that will increase the likelihood the learner will engage in this behavior a second time. The subsequent stimulation (reinforcement) from using the drug will most likely result in the individual's engaging in this behavior again and again. Similarly, a learner who gains positive sensory stimulation as a result of any behavior will probably demonstrate the behavior again to gain that same stimulation.

Another example is a child with autism spectrum disorder who persistently spins a reflective top on the floor. The child appears excited and enthralled with the flickering light and rotating top. It is difficult to engage her in another task or activity while the top is spinning. To pull the child away, the instructor must redirect her to another activity and put the top in a place where it is not visible to the child. When given a chance, the child will consistently choose to spin the top. Sensory stimulation may be used to (a) obtain reinforcement from internal stimulation or (b) obtain reinforcement from external stimulation. The following are examples of gaining sensory stimulation:

1. Johnny constantly hums while working on academic assignments.
2. Nikko chews on the tips of her pens or pencils while working on independent seatwork.

3. Sherrie twirls her hair and wraps it around her fingers while she is working on assignments; she twists and pulls it tighter and tighter until she pulls it out.

4. When Billy is left alone, he bites his knuckle until it bleeds and continues to bite his hand until a staff member interrupts him.

Effectively addressing the unique needs of learners with challenging behaviors requires a clear understanding of the basic concepts of behavior as well as the circumstances in which the challenging behaviors occur. Identifying those events, situations, or people that trigger inappropriate behavior, and proactively doing something about it, increases the likelihood of positive outcomes.

Understanding Why Learners Misbehave

Learners with challenging behaviors continue to misbehave for various reasons. We will concentrate on some of the more important reasons—or triggers—for these behaviors, and look at what school personnel can do to change the situation. The first step is to thoroughly understand the relationship between learner behavior and setting conditions.

Settings and Antecedent Events That Might Influence Problem Behavior

Multiple factors may impact or influence a learner's behavior, and many are related to the instructional setting (classroom, tasks, staff, schedule, peers, etc.). These factors are easy to change or manipulate. Other factors (sickness, medications, home problems, etc.) are more difficult or sometimes impossible to control. It is, however, critical to be aware of these factors and to understand the impact they may have on the learner's behavior.

The following is a short list of those factors that might influence the relationship between the learner's behavior and the environment.

• *Physiological factors.* Examples include sickness, allergies, side effects of medication, fatigue, hunger or thirst, increased arousal due to a fight, or a disruptive routine.

• *Home environment.* Examples include lack of supervision, inconsistent or insufficient home routine, highly punitive parenting style, insufficient resources to support learning, or an overly controlling parenting style.

Additional factors that might influence a learner's behavior might be more manageable and easier to control within the instructional setting; educators can provide accommodations and modifications to address the behavioral concerns. The following list provides some of the possible causes that may be considered when difficult behaviors occur.

• *Classroom environment.* Examples include high noise level, uncomfortable temperature, poor lighting, over- or understimulation, poor seating arrangement, frequent disruptions, lack of sufficient positive reinforcement, punitive or inconsistent discipline procedures, inappropriate or inadequate classroom rules and expectations, ineffective home–school communication, lack of predictability in the schedule, or inconsistent monitoring of progress.

• *Curriculum and instruction.* Examples include few opportunities for making choices, few opportunities for successful practice of skills, poor instructional pacing (too fast or too slow), inadequate level of assistance provided to the learner, unclear directions provided for activity completion, few opportunities for the learner to communicate, activities that are too difficult, activities that take a long time to complete, activities that the learner dislikes, activities for which the completion criterion is unclear, or activities that may not be perceived as being relevant or useful by the learner (Alberto & Troutman, 2006; Kazdin, 2001).

Measuring Learner Behavior

Data collection and behavior observation are important components of a special education program for two reasons. First, data collection and behavior observation provide an objective basis for making decisions and documenting learner behaviors and performance, and they make instructors' decisions more accurate and reliable. Second, when completed systematically, data collection can also provide consistent information on learner progress.

Although teams would prefer to have a "quick fix" in dealing with difficult behaviors, it is more efficient and effective in the long run to first understand and agree on the targeted behaviors prior to implementing any type of intervention plans. Specific descriptions of the behavior allow us to

1. have better communication among the instructional team, other colleagues, and families;
2. ensure that we are consistently observing and counting the exact same behaviors prior to and during intervention;
3. determine the most effective interventions to use in developing behavior plans;
4. more accurately measure learner progress;
5. have better access to important information and to the research literature; and
6. provide feedback and reinforcement to learners.

Why Do We Measure Behavior?

When examining the seriousness of a learner's inappropriate behaviors, it is important to accurately picture the actions. Equally important is to assess the appropriate behaviors related to the inappropriate behaviors that are causing difficulties for the learner and instructional team. It is also critical to understand the methods for collecting the data needed to obtain the relevant information. This will help to clarify the details of the situation prior to developing an intervention plan. Without an accurate picture of the learner's behavior, we cannot choose the correct tools and most effective interventions to address the situation.

In order to be *measurable,* a behavior must first be *observable* (Baer et al., 1968). In addition, the observer must be able to clearly determine when a specific behavior is occurring and count the occurrences of the behavior or time the duration of the behavior. Behaviors that have a distinct beginning and ending are the easiest to measure.

Why Do We Describe Behavior?

We describe behavior, using specific language, so that we can measure it accurately. To accurately measure and assess behaviors, we must first develop an *operational definition,* which includes a label and a specific description of the exact behavior that we have targeted. It is important to describe only what we can *see* and *count.* When developing an operational definition, it is essential to disregard any assumptions or biases about what the learner is feeling or why the learner is demonstrating the particular behavior (e.g., not doing homework because he is lazy, does not care, or is irresponsible; being disruptive because she is angry or dislikes the instructor; Skinner, 1953). The use of terms that are broad and vague in their definitions (e.g., *disrespectful, uncooperative, disruptive*) may also cause confusion or disagreement about whether the behavior is occurring. All team members, and others working with the learner, must agree on a label and a specific description of the behaviors. The information collected must be as accurate as possible. To obtain accurate data, the observation procedure must remain consistent from one observation to another and from one observer to another, and it must decrease the chance for errors. The following considerations are important in implementing a data-collection system and behavior observations. To be effective, a data-collection system must include

1. a clear definition of the behaviors to be observed and measured;
2. a clear description of the data-collection procedure, including a well-organized recording system; and
3. an opportunity for the observer to learn and practice the observation technique.

A data-recording system must provide enough information to make the observation useful but easy enough to not interfere with the observation. This is a critical consideration when selecting the tools for measuring learner behavior.

Selecting Measurement Tools and Observation Techniques

In determining the data-collection technique to use, we must take into consideration the specific behavior and the information we are attempting to gain from the observation. It is the supervisor's responsibility to determine which data-collection technique to use; however, as a paraeducator, you will need to understand these techniques and have a chance to practice them before using them in an observation. The following are brief descriptions of various data-collection methods.

Frequency Count

When using a frequency count, the observer records the number of times a specific behavior occurs within a specific time period. Frequency counts are useful for recording behaviors that have a clear beginning and ending, are of relatively short duration, and occur fairly frequently during a specified time period. In order to use the frequency count method, the following are necessary.

1. An available specific time period
2. A well-defined behavior
3. A recording method for tracking the number of occurrences of the behavior
4. A recording or tally sheet to record the frequency with which or the number of times that the specific behavior occurs

Following are examples of how the frequency of a behavior might be recorded:

1. The number of times a learner raises his or her hand during a 15-minute group lesson
2. The number of multiplication problems completed on a worksheet within 5 minutes
3. The number of times a learner leaves his or her seat during history class

A frequency count should *not* be used for behaviors that occur at a high rate or many, many times, such as tapping a pencil on a desk or rocking a chair. Also, it should *not* be used when the behavior occurs over an extended period of time, such as when a learner cries.

Rate

Calculating a rate is similar to tallying frequency of events. Calculating a behavioral rate takes into account both data on the frequency of the observed behavior and the length of the observation time. Rate is the ratio of the number of times a behavior occurs within a specific time period and the length of the time period. The rate is computed by dividing the number of events or frequency by the number of minutes, hours, or days over which the observation occurred. For example, if a learner was out of his seat five times in a 20-minute reading session, you would divide 5 by 20 (5/20) to determine his rate per minute. In this case, the learner's rate of out-of-seat behavior is .25 per minute. A learner's average rate of behavioral occurrences over time can be determined from a series of observations by adding the rates for each observation (e.g., .25 + .33 + .20 + 1.0 = 1.78) and dividing by the total number of observations (4). In this example the learner's average rate of out-of-seat behavior over time is .45 per minute.

Duration

The duration of a behavior is found by recording the exact starting and ending time of a behavior and then computing the length of time the behavior occurs. This technique is usually used to observe behaviors that occur less frequently and continue over a substantial period of time.

An example of duration recording is when a learner has incidences of crying in class. Each time the learner cries in class, the observer records the beginning and ending times and then calculates the duration of the crying incident. Additional examples of behaviors appropriate for duration recording are the length of time a learner stays on task, the length of time a learner takes to transition to a new activity, or the length of time a learner continuously taps his or her pencil on the desk.

Interval Recording

Interval recording is a technique that measures whether a behavior occurs within a specific time interval. The observation time is divided into small intervals, and the observer records whether the behavior occurs within that short interval. By using the interval recording technique, an estimate of both the frequency and duration of the behavior can be obtained. If the specific behavior occurs at any time within the interval, the observer records the behavior only once. Because the observation is continuous for a set period of time, interval recording demands the observer's complete attention.

An example of a behavior for which interval recording could be used is talking to peers during independent work time. If the work time lasts for 15 minutes, that time can be broken into five 3-minute intervals. If in the first interval the learner talks to her neighbor, the interval is marked (possibly using a plus sign). If the learner is working quietly during the next interval, the interval is not marked. If in the third interval the child talks to three different learners, the interval is marked again, only once. At the end of the data-collection period, the data are summarized by counting the number of intervals in which the behavior occurred and placing it over the total number of intervals (e.g., talk-outs occurred for three out of the five intervals, or 3/5).

Anecdotal Records

Anecdotal records are a written description of events or incidents. The purpose of an anecdotal record is to document an event as clearly and precisely as possible. If a paraeducator is working with the learner at the time of a specific incident, she or he may be asked to assist in completing an anecdotal record of the event. Anecdotal records are often used to document (a) a significant event that occurs infrequently or unexpectedly, (b) the settings or conditions in which a specific behavior occurred, and (c) the antecedents to (what happens before) and the consequences of (what happens after) a problem behavior.

The following guidelines are helpful when writing an anecdotal record:

1. Record descriptions of the incident as soon as possible after the behavior is observed.
2. Have a standardized anecdotal record form to record the information and to help ensure that (a) all relevant information is included, and (b) you record what is *actually observed* rather than your feelings about the incident.

A Model for Describing and Pinpointing Behaviors

It is important to practice labeling and defining behaviors, observing behaviors, and using various recording techniques to increase accuracy of observation and recording. Use of observation and data-collection techniques gets easier over time. Keeping it simple will help to ensure that a data-collection system will be implemented consistently to gain necessary information about learners. The following is a summary and model for developing a system of data collection.

1. Determine an appropriate label for the behavior (e.g., aggression, off-task, poor work completion).
   - Must be representative of the behavior
   - Must be short and concise (the description will be more lengthy and specific)
2. Develop an operational definition (i.e., ask yourself, "What does the behavior look like or sound like?").
3. Determine the best method for measuring the behavior.
   - How many times does it occur (i.e., *Frequency* = #TIMES or *Rate* = #TIMES per TIME PERIOD)?
   - How long (i.e., *Duration* = HOW LONG does the behavior LAST)?
   - Is it important to gain information about both the frequency and the duration of the behavior (i.e., *Interval Recording* = Does the behavior occur at any point during a short interval)?
   - Is there additional important information about the behavior that must be gathered (i.e., *Anecdotal Records* = Specific description of an event)?

The following are additional considerations for implementing a data-collection system.

1. Data-collection procedures should not cause a distraction from instruction.
2. Data-collection procedures should not take excessive amounts of time away from instruction.
3. Results of data collection should lead to modifications and improvements in instructional programming.
4. The observer should respect the privacy and dignity of learners.

The Paraeducator's Role in Data Collection

The paraeducator plays an important role in gathering and organizing information about learner behavior. When a paraeducator's data collection is systematic and well organized, the teacher can make important instructional and programmatic decisions concerning a learner's behavior. When a paraeducator is knowledgeable about the process of collecting data, has been trained in the observation techniques, and has a clear understanding of the behavior being observed, he or she can easily perform behavioral observations.

Positive Behavior Supports: Setting Up the Learning Environment for Success

Your instructional team must take time to develop a thoughtful plan to maximize the learner's potential for success. Most learners come to a setting anticipating direction on the classroom limits, rules, consequences, and expectations. Successful educators take this opportunity to lay out a clear and specific plan that will guide the learners and make the classroom predictable and the system thoroughly understood. Several factors are critical to ensure that your preparations are complete. The following are some of the important components of an effective positive behavior support plan (Madsen & Thomas, 1986).

Rules and Expectations

You must first ask the question, "What do I expect from learners—both behaviorally and academically?" If you waiver in your expectations, hour to hour or day to day, your learners will be constantly confused and unsettled; on the other hand, if the expectations are clear, the learner comes into the situation knowing exactly what will happen. The primary issue is to determine classroom expectations and, in addition, write down those expectations and post them for all to see.

Activity: Write down five expectations for behavior and five expectations for academic performance that you expect to see from learners. Remember to write them in terms that are observable and measurable (those that you can see and count). For example, "I expect the learners to come to class on time (in their seats when the bell rings) and to be prepared with materials (paper, pencil, and book)."

Rules are an essential component of a winning classroom. Developing rules is much easier when personal expectations are clarified for the learners. Now, prioritize the expectations that you wrote in the activity. Use the most important expectations to begin to develop your rules. Keep in mind that the rules must reflect *your* expectations. For example, if it is not important to you to have learners raise their hands to speak or if you are not willing to follow through with the consequences *consistently*, do not include that behavior in your rules. Having rules that are inconsistently enforced gives learners the idea that rules are not important or that there will not be a consequence. This leads to increased rates of inappropriate behavior.

Rhode, Jenson, and Reavis (1992) have developed a set of guidelines for developing classroom rules that help to ensure that the rules are stated in the most effective and efficient way possible.

1. *Keep it positive. Rules should be stated using positive language.* Make sure that the rules are telling the learners what they should DO, not what they should NOT DO. For example,

Instead of	Use
Do not talk!	Listen to the instructor with a quiet mouth.
Don't run in the halls!	Walk in the halls at all times.
No fighting!	Keep your hands, feet, and objects to yourself.
Don't talk out!	Raise your hand quietly and wait to be called on to speak.

2. *Keep it short and simple.* Having a lot of rules does not necessarily mean that learners will be better behaved. In fact, it may have the opposite effect. Having five to six rules assists learners in knowing and understanding the rules clearly.

3. *Keep it clear. Write the rules using language that describes* observable *and* measurable *behaviors.* It is important that the behaviors referred to in your rules are clearly stated. When writing your rules, it is best to refrain from using terms that are unclear or vague; words like *respect, responsibility,* or *appropriate* can be problematic. These words are difficult to define, have meanings that vary from individual to individual, and are often misinterpreted. It is best to avoid using terms like these and, instead, think about what *respect* looks and sounds like. If you find that you must use a word that may not have a clear meaning, be sure to clarify in

the learners' minds by thoroughly explaining the meaning of the rule. For example, if you have followed the first guideline and…

Instead of	You Choose to Use
No cursing!	Use only positive and acceptable language.

you must first *teach* the learners exactly what positive and acceptable language *is* and *is not*.

4. *Include a compliance rule.* Having a compliance or following-directions rule is critical. Developing compliance in learners will help to get rid of many unwanted behaviors before they have a chance to get going. Many behaviors stem from learners' ignoring or delaying a request given by an adult and then arguing or throwing a tantrum. If the learner causes too much of a fuss, the adult will often give in, just to get the learner to stop. A coercive behavior chain looks like the following:

Adult	Child
Are you ready to get to work?	(learner ignores)
Come on! Let's get your math done, okay?	I need to finish my reading first.
How many times do I need to tell you? If I tell you again, you will stay in for recess!	This work is too hard. You won't help me! I hate school!
That's it! You've lost your recesses today!	(learner tantrums)
Okay, I've had it! Go sit in the hallway!	(learner stops the tantrum and leaves)

We all get caught up in this type of interaction at some time, whether at school or at home with our own kids. If the teacher had had a compliance rule in place, there would have been an automatic consequence for *not* following the rules the first time, and the situation may not have escalated to a point of no return. Having a compliance rule also gives the instructor an opportunity to provide learners with positive reinforcement for following directions, which in turn encourages them to follow directions in order to gain some type of reward or praise. In the long run, learners will see the benefits and success that following directions brings. Compliance is essential in ensuring success in and outside of a classroom.

5. *Teach the rules, using examples and nonexamples (and review often).* In the first few weeks of school, it is important for the instructional team to devote a portion of the school day to teaching and reviewing the rules. Teaching the rules includes providing

- clear explanations and descriptions of what the rule means;
- a rationale for the rule (why is it important?);
- lots of examples (what does it look like?) and nonexamples (what does it *not* look like?)—this is best done with modeling;
- opportunities for role-playing scenarios to practice the rules; and
- positive feedback and reinforcement for following the rules.

The initial investment in taking the time and energy to teach the rules will pay off. After the first couple of weeks, the learners will know the rules well, and they will be fully aware of making the choice to either follow or not follow the rules.

6. *Clearly state consequences, both positive and negative.* The learners must know what will happen when they do or do not follow the rules. The consequences should reflect the events that will occur and, when appropriate, the time and place in which the consequence will take effect.

7. *Rules and consequences should be posted for all to see.* Have you ever been in a situation in which you see a policeman and are unsure of the speed limit in the area? What is the first thing you do? First, you check your speed (your behavior) and then you look for a posted sign. The same applies to learners. Posted rules and consequences remind learners of the limits and also bring about a "check your own behavior" response. This step prompts not only learners but also teachers and staff to remember the rules and expectations.

Activity: An instructor has the following five rules posted on the wall:

1. Follow directions given by adults within 10 seconds.

2. Raise your hand and wait to be called on to speak.

3. Come to class prepared with book, papers, pencil, and homework.

4. Be in your seat when the bell rings.

5. Use positive and appropriate language.

Both positive and negative consequences are also posted. The instructor taught the meaning of the rules and used role-plays and coaching in the first weeks of the school year. Every learner in the class can repeat all five rules. Consequences are consistently implemented for *most* of the rules, *most* of the time. However, the teacher finds that the learners often make comments or call out answers without raising their hands during a class discussion. This is becoming a problem.

Discuss the following:

• Are the teacher's rules effective? Do they follow the stated guidelines?
• What is going wrong? What are some reasons that the teacher is having a problem with learners talking out without raising their hands?
• What could the teacher do to change the situation?

Instructional Considerations

Often, when a learner engages in behavioral problems, we take the behavior personally. In other words, we see the behavior as a statement about how the learner feels about us. It is important to take into consideration other factors that may significantly affect the learner's daily life. Much of the behavior we see in school stems from academic difficulties. When problems arise, answering these questions might help to pinpoint factors that could be contributing to a problem situation, in regard to one particular learner or to an entire group. Considering the answers to these questions will also assist teams in designing effective behavior intervention plans (Munk & Repp, 1994).

Choice of tasks

• Does the learner or the instructor select most of the activities?
• Does the learner have identifiable preferences for tasks or activities?
• Does problem behavior occur more often when the instructor assigns tasks?
• Does the learner express a preference for alternative tasks when the instructor presents a task?
• Does the problem behavior result in a change in tasks or activities? Is the learner allowed to select an alternative task?
• If allowed to select tasks, does the learner select one or two tasks, or several tasks?

Task variation

- How many tasks are available within 5, 10, 15, 30, and 60 minutes of instruction?
- Does problem behavior increase as time on a single task increases?
- Does the learner stop the assigned task and begin other activities during an instructional period?
- Does the learner display fewer problem behaviors during brief tasks?

Pace of instruction

- Does problem behavior occur while the instructor is providing instruction (i.e., during a lesson) or between lessons?
- What is the average number of instructional commands presented in 1 minute?
- Does the learner engage in off-task behavior such as gazing, leaving seat, or other inappropriate behaviors during instruction?

Reduced task difficulty

- Does problem behavior occur more often after correct responding or after incorrect responding?
- Does the learner require frequent prompts to respond?
- How often does the instructor reinforce learner responses, whether correct or incorrect?
- Does the learner spend more time performing easy activities?
- Can the instructor predict which tasks will produce increased inappropriate behavior?

Answering these questions can prove helpful when behaviors are occurring consistently and becoming more frequent or more intense. Overall, remembering the ABCs, looking for patterns in behaviors, and considering that the instruction or tasks may be a contributing factor will help to keep problems in check.

Teaching Replacement Behaviors

A replacement behavior is an alternative to the problem behavior—the behavior we want the learner to use *in place of* the inappropriate behavior. Identifying replacement or alternative behaviors is one of the most important components of a positive behavior support plan. When you observe and understand why a problem behavior is occurring, you must also pinpoint the new behavior you want the person to perform. The most effective way to identify replacement behaviors is to meet as a team with individuals who are familiar with the learner and brainstorm possible ideas for the replacement behavior. The more ideas you get, the better the chance that you will find one that will be successful. It is important to identify a behavior that is the *opposite* of the problem behavior; that way, the learner will not likely be able to exhibit both behaviors at the same time. For example, the learner cannot have a *quiet* hand-raise and talk out at the same time, or the learner cannot have hands in pockets and hit another learner at the same time. Remember, you cannot extinguish a difficult behavior without teaching the learner a more appropriate behavior with which to replace it.

The following are several general guidelines for successfully teaching replacement behaviors:

- The replacement behavior must have the same outcome as the problem behavior. If the learner is using an inappropriate behavior to gain attention, the new behavior must also get him or her attention.
- The replacement behavior must receive positive reinforcement as soon as, or sooner than, the problem behavior.
- The replacement behavior must receive *at least* as much reinforcement as the problem behavior.
- The replacement behavior must be as fluent as the problem behavior (i.e., the replacement behavior must be rehearsed over and over to make sure the learner is able to perform the behavior when necessary).

These skills must be taught systematically and effectively, providing learners with ample opportunities to practice and rehearse the skills both inside and outside of the classroom. Systematic instruction involves using effective skill instruction, breaking down tasks into smaller and easier portions, using appropriate teaching methods, and rewarding and correct-ing behaviors consistently.

A few of the most effective teaching strategies are modeling, prompt-ing, shaping, and fading. When teaching a learner a new skill, such as making polite comments, it is important to model the behavior first. Mod-eling is demonstrating a new behavior so that a learner might acquire the skill by observing it. Typically you provide several examples of what the behavior looks and sounds like to help the learner easily identify the skill when he or she hears it named in conversation. Modeling is essential, whether teaching an academic skill or classroom behavior.

Next the learner must practice the behavior. A skilled instructor uses prompting to encourage a student to try out a new behavior. Prompting comes in many forms and may be carried out visually, verbally, physically, or via a combination of all three. For example, if you are teaching the learner to make a polite comment on the playground, you might verbally prompt him to approach another child who has fallen by pointing to the fallen child and asking "What can you say or do to help?" Once the learner thinks of what to say, prompt him to talk to the child. Do not forget to praise him, and keep in mind that the polite comment does not have to be perfect. It's a beginning.

Another teaching strategy that goes hand in hand with prompting is shaping. Shaping consists of systematically reinforcing a learner's approxi-mations of the desired behavior until the learner can demonstrate the behavior successfully over time. You may think about it as baby steps to reach the target behavior. For example, if you are encouraging a student to interact with her peers at recess, you might first reinforce her for play-ing next to students on the playground, then for watching the students play, and finally for asking if she can join the group. Asking others to play can be difficult for a child who is shy or withdrawn, so remember to sup-port the learner's efforts using prompts and plenty of reinforcement. Once the learner is successfully asking others to play, withdraw the prompts and gradually fade or decrease your reinforcement over time until the child is engaging others on the playground without your assistance.

When an Individual Knows How To Perform a Skill but Does Not

There may be several reasons why a person does not use the appropriate skill when the situation calls for it. First, the individual may not recognize the social or environmental cues that should prompt the use of the skill. Second, the skill may *not* be as efficient or effective as the problem behavior (e.g., problem behavior gets reinforced more immediately or consistently or requires less effort), and the learner may rely on old habits to get the desired outcome. Additionally, there may be other variables that are influencing behavior in certain situations (e.g., distractions, discomfort).

Positive Reinforcement

Researchers have long identified reinforcement as an effective strategy in improving the conduct of children and youth. To understand how positive reinforcement works, we must first understand what it is. Positive reinforcement involves the *contingent* presentation of a consequence that increases the likelihood of a behavior occurring again (Skinner, 1953). For it to act as a reinforcer, the consequence must immediately follow the behavior and be something that is valued or desired by the learner. For example, when Larry completed his work, his teacher immediately gave him 5 points and some extra free time with a friend. Thereafter, Larry continued to complete his work on time so that he could earn extra time with his best friend. In this case, the extra free time acted as a reinforcer. How do we know? By looking at Larry's behavior. Did it increase or decrease? Reinforcement has occurred only if the target behavior (i.e., Larry's task completion) increases or stays the same.

Positive reinforcement comes in many forms but primarily includes

- verbal praise,
- social praise,
- access to preferred activities,
- access to material items, and
- access to people.

How Do You Select Reinforcement?

Selecting reinforcement is easy. Learners typically give us many clues if we just take the time to observe or listen to them. The following are some excellent ideas for determining possible reinforcement:

- What does the learner like to do in his or her free time?
- What does the learner do most often?

- What does the learner talk about?
- What would the learner like to earn?

For learners who are unable to express their preferences by using verbal communication, reinforcer-sampling procedures can be used:

- Let the learner sample some possible reinforcers to determine his or her preference.
- Let the learner pick from a list or menu of reinforcers.
- Review what has worked in the past.

Keep in mind the Golden Rule for selecting reinforcers: "the cheaper, the faster, the better." That is, when your teacher and you are selecting reinforcement, make sure it is inexpensive, easy to provide (i.e., does not take a lot of staff time), and natural whenever possible (Hall & Hall, 1980).

When To Provide Positive Reinforcement

To increase the effectiveness of reinforcement, the following are a few simple rules—frequently referred to as the IFEEDAV rules—to remember (Rhode et al., 1992):

I   immediate

F   frequent

E   enthusiastic

E   eye contact

D   describe

A   anticipation

V   variety

Let's briefly talk about each:

Deliver reinforcement immediately

Reinforcement must occur immediately following the target behavior. The longer the delay between the occurrence of the desired behavior and the reinforcer, the greater the likelihood that another, less desirable behavior may be reinforced and the less effective the reinforcer will be.

Deliver reinforcement frequently

Reinforce often. This is particularly important when you are teaching a new behavior or skill to a learner. Experts recommend maintaining a ratio of four positive reinforcers for every negative consequence. That might sound high, but giving reinforcement is as simple as winking at a learner or thanking him or her for raising a hand quietly.

Be enthusiastic

When you give a reinforcer, it is critical that you are enthusiastic and sincere. Learners can immediately detect if you are less than interested in what they are doing by what you say and how you say it. Although it takes more effort on your part, it is generally worth it.

Make eye contact

When giving a reinforcer, it is important to look the learner directly in the eyes. This conveys the message to the learner that he or she is important and that your reinforcer is sincere.

Describe the behavior

It is commonly said that "we get more of what we reinforce." If we specifically describe or tell the learner what we like about his or her behavior, it will increase the likelihood that the desired behavior will happen again. For example, the statement "Thanks for taking your seat quietly" conveys to the learner much more about the specific looked-for behavior when he or she enters the classroom than the statement "Good job." Do not assume that learners know what they have done well. Tell them.

Create anticipation

Build anticipation about your reinforcers. The more excitement you can generate about the reinforcers, the more motivated your learners will be to earn them.

Use a variety of reinforcers

Just because you are using a high rate of reinforcers does not mean that they all have to look and sound alike. All adults and learners get bored with the same reinforcer over time (e.g., a pop or a candy bar). The greater the variety, the higher the learner's interest level and motivation, so rotate your reinforcers often or provide the learner with a menu of reinforcers from which to choose. Plan ahead. Develop a "bank" of reinforcer options with your supervisor to have on hand during instruction or free time, and do not forget to pair a positive praise statement with each tangible or material reinforcer that you provide.

Types of Reinforcers

There are several types of reinforcement, including material, edible, social, and natural (Rhode et al., 1992). A brief description of these types of reinforcement follows.

Material reinforcement
Material reinforcement consists of some tangible item that a learner can earn for practicing a preferred behavior. Tangible items may include stickers, jewelry, pencils, art supplies, and so forth. As you and your supervisor generate ideas for tangible reinforcers, remember to keep the items affordable.

Edible reinforcers
Edible reinforcers are just that—something you prefer to eat. Common forms of edible reinforcers include ice cream, pop, fruit, pretzels, gummy bears, popcorn, carrot sticks, french fries, and M & M's. When selecting edible reinforcers, you must pay attention to a learner's specific dietary needs. Check with the learner's parents and your team prior to using *any* edible reinforcers.

Social reinforcement
Any verbal statement, positive attention, or action made by the instructor that increases or maintains a learner's desired behavior such as a smile, a wink, a pat on the back, or telling a learner, "That was so awesome. You did just what I asked, and quickly too!" is an example of social reinforcement. Pairing social reinforcement with other forms of reinforcement, such as edibles, helps to build the value of the social reinforcement, especially for those learners who initially may not find praise motivating.

Natural positive reinforcers
Natural reinforcers are everywhere in our schools; we just need to know how to recognize and use them to our advantage. Such activities as

"being the instructor's helper," "tutoring another learner," "erasing the board," "running a note to the office," "being in charge of the class hamster," or "helping the custodian" are powerful motivators for most learners. Too often we give these activities away without recognizing their potential to change a learner's behavior. Better yet, all of the activities listed are free and require only a little forethought on the part of you and your supervisor.

Things To Remember

There are a few things to consider when using reinforcement with your learners. First, the reinforcers should be age appropriate. Be sure to discuss the reinforcement ideas with your supervisor and inform the learner's parents prior to using a specific reinforcer. Also, do not forget Grandma's Law, or the Premack Principle (Premack, 1959): Grandmothers have always known best. For example, grandmothers always say, "First do your homework, then you can go out and play." For reinforcement to truly work, it must follow the desired behavior, not precede it.

Teaching Strategies for Increasing Compliance

In today's schools, learners are expected to follow multiple directions given to them throughout the day. How you make a request can make a huge difference in how often your learners comply with it. Research has shown that if requests are given correctly, you can increase compliance by 30% (Forehand, 1977).

The following are ways to increase the effectiveness of your directions. If used correctly, you will have fewer problems, less arguing, and more compliance in your classroom.

• *Don't ask if it isn't a question.* Using a direct request increases the possibility that the leaner will follow through. For example, "I need you to sit in your chair" is more effective than asking, "Will you sit in this seat, please?"

• *Get up close.* If you want compliance, it is far better to give a request up close than from a distance. Three feet or the length of your arm is typically recommended. Being closer to a learner when making a request increases the chance that he or she will follow directions.

• *Use eye contact.* Look the learner in the eye as you give an instruction. Be sure to say his or her name and request that the learner look you in the eye before you give the request.

• *Give one request at a time.* Avoid asking a learner to do multiple tasks all at once. Give only one request at a time, wait for the learner to follow through, and then give another request.

• *Use a quiet, calm voice.* Don't yell.

• *Get close and stay cool.* When giving a direction, get up close and use a calm, nonemotional voice when stating the request. Raising your voice or threatening the learner will only increase his or her noncompliance.

• *Don't nag.* Make a request only twice. State the request once, wait 3 to 5 seconds, and then restate the same request. If the learner does not follow through, put a mild consequence in place.

• *Give the learner time.* After making a request, allow 5 seconds for the learner to comply before repeating the request or giving a new request.

• *Be specific and descriptive.* It helps to give specific requests rather than global requests. Descriptive requests increase the likelihood that learners will understand exactly what you want them to do and increases the chance of their success. For example, "Get your work done" is vague. "Please complete all of the problems at the bottom of page 2" pinpoints the exact actions you want the learner to take.

• *Verbally reinforce compliance.* Don't forget to praise the learner when he or she follows through with your request. Remember, you get more of what you reinforce.

• *Use precision commands.* One strategy that has been found to significantly increase learner compliance is precision commands. A precision command (see Figure 4.1), sometimes referred to as a "precision request," is a precise verbal statement made by staff members to enhance learner compliance (Hamlet, Axelrod, & Kuerschner, 1984; Rhode et al., 1992; Utah State Office of Education, 2001).

A precision command consists of a two-step format. When giving a precision command, directions are stated positively and given to a learner in a clear and concise manner each time. The first step consists of making a polite request such as, "Deb, please pick up your toys and put them in the box." Because descriptive commands are more effective than ambiguous or general commands, it is important to describe the specific behavior

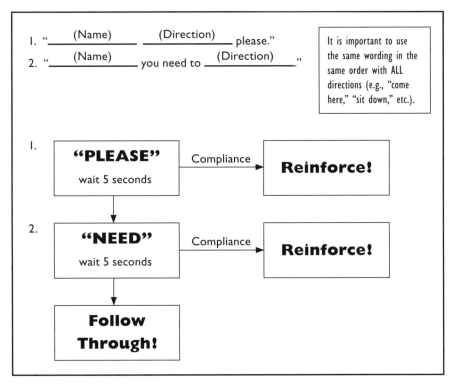

Figure 4.1. Two-step precision command format.

using a soft but firm, nonemotional voice. Do not yell. After giving the precision command, allow the learner 3 to 5 seconds to comply. Frequently, instructors unnecessarily repeat the command or give a new command before the learner has had time to comply with the original command. If the learner complies, praise him or her. However, if the learner fails to comply, give a second command.

The second command is more effective if warning words such as *need* and *now* are used to signal to the learner that, unless he or she complies, an unpleasant consequence will follow. For example, "Deb, you need to place all of the toys in the box now." Again, following the second command, allow the learner 3 to 5 seconds to comply. If the learner has not started to respond after the second command, follow through with a preplanned, unpleasant consequence, such as a loss of recess time or free time. As a team, discuss a hierarchy of possible unpleasant consequences to use if a learner fails to comply with the second command. Following the unpleasant consequence, restate the second command and praise the learner when he or she complies with your request.

Keep in mind it is important to use the same wording in the same order with all directions that you give. Another key to increasing compliance is to give the learner an appropriate amount of time to respond to the request. The general guidelines are to allow 3 to 5 seconds for learners who *do not* have language difficulties to respond, and allow 7 to 10 seconds for learners who *do* have language difficulties or auditory processing problems. Also, praise learners for following directions. Positive attention should always be given when learners comply with requests.

Summary

This chapter examined the paraeducator's role in the effective management of learner behavior and discussed a few of the proven management practices that work. Understanding why behavior occurs within a particular setting is key to designing effective management programs for all learners. As a paraeducator, it is your role to become familiar with your supervisor's management plan or schoolwide plan and assist in implementing effective, proactive management strategies on a day-to-day basis.

ACTIVITIES

1. Make a list of your classroom rules and expectations. Evaluate your rules according to the seven guidelines for establishing effective rules. Ask yourself if they are positively stated. If they are not, rewrite the rules based on what you know is best practice.

2. List one or two replacement behaviors for each behavior listed. Keep in mind the likely reasons for the behavior.
   - Problem behavior: Hitting
     Reasons for hitting: Gets angry and does not know what else to do when others tease him or her
     Replacement Behavior(s):

   - Problem behavior: Noncompliance
     Reasons for noncompliance: Gets out of doing work; receives

instructor's attention
Replacement behavior(s):

- Problem behavior: Off-task behavior
Reasons for off-task behavior: Lacks skills to do two-digit addition
Replacement behavior(s):

- Problem behavior: Teasing others
Reasons for teasing others: Wants peer attention
Replacement behavior(s):

Discussion Questions

1. Why is it important to use positive behavior management strategies?

2. Describe the components of an effective behavior management plan.

3. Discuss the paraeducator's role in implementing a classroom behavior management plan.

4. List and describe three strategies that paraeducators can use to decrease inappropriate behavior.

5. List and describe three strategies that paraeducators can use to increase appropriate behavior.

6. A learner is repeatedly teasing another child at recess. What might you do?

7. List the ways to increase the effectiveness of positive verbal praise.

8. List and describe the essential components for observing and understanding difficult behaviors.

References

Alberto, P. A., & Troutman, A. C. (2006). *Applied behavior analysis procedures for teachers* (7th ed.). Englewood Cliffs, NJ: Prentice Hall.

Baer, D. M., Wolf, M. M., & Risley, T. R. (1968). Some current dimensions of applied behavior analysis. *Journal of Applied Behavior Analysis, 1,* 91–97.

Carr, E., & Durand, M. (1985). Reducing behavior problems through functional communication training. *Journal of Applied Behavior Analysis, 18,* 111–126.

Forehand, R. (1977). Child noncompliance to parental commands: Behavior analysis and treatment. In M. Hersen, R. M. Eisler, & P. M. Miller (Eds.), *Progress in behavior modification* (Vol. 5, pp. 111–147). New York: Academic Press.

Hall, R. V., & Hall, M. C. (1980). *How to select reinforcers.* Lawrence, KS: H&H Enterprises.

Hamlet, C. C., Axelrod, S., & Kuerschner, S. (1984). Eye contact as an antecedent to compliant behavior. *Journal of Applied Behavior Analysis, 17,* 553–557.

Kazdin, A. E. (2001). *Behavior modification in applied settings* (6th ed.). Belmont, CA: Wadsworth/Thomson Learning.

Latham, G. (2000). Behavior strategies that work. *Utah Special Educator, 20*(3), 7–10.

Madsen, C. H., & Thomas, D. R. (1986). Rules, praise, and ignoring: Elements of elementary classroom control. *Journal of Applied Behavior Analysis, 1,* 139–150.

Mish, F. C. (Ed.). (1998). *Merriam-Webster's collegiate dictionary* (10th ed.). Springfield, MA: Merriam-Webster.

Munk, D. D., & Repp, A. C. (1994). The relationship between instructional variables and problem behavior: A review. *Exceptional Children, 60,* 390–401.

O'Neill, R., Horner, R., Albin, R., Sprague, J., Storey, K., & Newton, J. S. (1997). *Functional assessment and program development for problem behavior* (2nd ed.). Pacific Grove, CA: Brooks/Cole.

Premack, D. (1959). Toward empirical behavior laws: I. Positive reinforcement. *Psychological Review, 66,* 219–233.

Rhode, G., Jenson, W., & Reavis, H. K. (1992). *The tough kid book: Practical classroom management strategies.* Longmont, CO: Sopris West.

Skinner, B. F. (1953). *Science and human behavior.* New York: Macmillan.

U. S. Office of Special Edu. Programs. (1999). *Applying positive behavioral support and functional behavioral assessment in schools.* Retrieved October 20, 2005, from http://www.pbis.org/researchLiterature.htm

Utah State Office of Education. (2001). *Precision commands least restrictive behavioral interventions (LRBI) video training program.* Salt Lake City: Author.

The Importance of Paraeducator Preparation and Ongoing Development

5

Teri Wallace

. . . .

Many paraeducators working in schools across the country report that they receive little or no preparation or ongoing training related to the work they do with students. This lack of development can lead to feelings of incompetence, worry about doing something wrong, and an ineffective role as a classroom team member. Conversely, those who report that they do receive training also report feeling competent in their day-to-day work with students. It is clear that initial preparation and ongoing development is critical for paraeducators to feel and be successful in their roles in our nation's schools. This chapter provides information about preparation and ongoing training, policies that support paraeducator training, competencies and standards for training, strategies for documentation, and roles related to paraeducator training and development for those who direct the work of paraeducators.

Learning Objectives

The content of this chapter will prepare paraeducators to do the following:

1. Understand the importance of preparation for paraeducator roles and responsibilities and the legislation that supports it
2. Learn the importance of alignment between position definition, role, preparation and training, and assessment
3. Understand paraeducator knowledge and skill competencies

4. Develop a strategy for documenting training and development experiences
5. Understand the role of teachers who direct the work of paraeducators

Key Terms and Definitions

The following key terms and definitions will be used throughout this chapter.

Alignment. The arrangement of something in an orderly position related to something else (e.g., the training a paraeducator receives should be in alignment with his or her role and responsibilities)

Initial preparation. The training paraeducators receive *before* they begin working in their paraeducator role (e.g., college courses, workshops)

Ongoing development. Preparation and training that occurs during paraeducator employment and leads to career development or strengthening one's job-specific skills (e.g., workshops, on-the-job training, self-paced training, coaching)

Training. Job-related learning opportunities

Elements of Effective Training

Joyce and Showers (as cited in Pickett & Gerlach, 2003) stated that the most effective training has the following five key elements:

1. *Theory*—the reason behind the skill or strategy; why it is important and rationale for its importance; and clear description of the skills, strategy, or concept
2. *Demonstration*—experienced person shows the skill or strategy in a realistic setting
3. *Practice*—the paraeducator tries out the skill or applies the skill in a controlled setting
4. *Feedback*—a knowledgeable, experienced person tells the paraeducator what he or she is doing right and what should be done differently

5. *Coaching*—occurs on-the-job while the paraeducator is working with students and typically consists of verbal prompts or physical gestures, such as pointing

Although it is very important for staff development specialists, community college instructors, and supervising teachers to understand these elements, it is also very important for paraeducators to be aware of them. As adults, paraeducators can be partners in their own preparation and training. Consider the example provided in the following case study.

AMANDA

Amanda attended a summer workshop on using positive behavior supports for students with challenging behavior. She and her teacher felt that such training would be useful to Amanda. Although the instructors of the workshop did a good job of providing the theory behind the strategies and described the strategies well, they did not demonstrate them. When school began in the fall, Amanda explained to her supervising teacher that she had learned a great deal during the workshop. She asked her supervising teacher the following questions:

1. Would she be willing to provide Amanda with a demonstration of some of the strategies she had learned in the summer?

2. Could her supervising teacher take time to watch Amanda try the strategy with the students and give her feedback?

By asking her supervising teacher to assist her, Amanda will learn much more about implementing the skills and strategies she learned.

Some people believe that if they learn something once they should know it well enough to implement it. Sometimes people feel embarrassed if they have forgotten or did not fully understand something from a training session. Learning new strategies and how to apply them to the unique needs of students takes time and practice. It is important that teachers, administrators, and paraeducators understand and plan for frequent practice and feedback opportunities.

In addition to the elements of effective training identified by Joyce and Showers (1980), there are a number of guiding principles that might be used in designing training for paraeducators. Wallace (2003) suggested the following regarding paraeducator preparation and training opportunities:

1. The training should be aligned with a set of competencies and standards of performance.
2. Some training formats are more important than others for teaching certain skills. For example, an overview of the schoolwide behavioral plan might take place in a large group, but a behavior plan for a specific student with an Individualized Education Program (IEP) requires focused on-the-job training and modeling by a teacher.
3. Training should be comprehensive, allowing for various types of opportunities, and include specific instruction regarding the needs of the students with whom the paraeducator works.
4. Training opportunities should be built into a sustainable support system to allow for ongoing paraeducator development.
5. An initial orientation to the school and its procedures and programs must be followed and should provide opportunities for ongoing targeted training and supervision.
6. Training individuals in teacher and paraeducator teams on new strategies offers the team the opportunity to discuss appropriate implementation roles while learning the same content at the same time.
7. When paraeducators have received specific skill training, it is important to follow up and ensure that they implement the skill correctly. Positive feedback is essential to ensure appropriate use of the skill.
8. Training and preparation are important and must be aligned with appropriate role expectations and day-to-day supervision.

Paraeducator Roles and Responsibilities

The role of the paraeducator in the educational environment must first be established. The role of paraeducators is to *assist and support* the teaching and learning environment for students with whom they work. Paraeducators work with licensed staff to help students learn and grow. Paraeducators do not develop lesson plans or provide initial instruction, but they reinforce teacher-developed instruction with targeted students. The paraeducator role offers students additional adult interaction, increased instructional time and focus, one-on-one or small-group attention, and much, much more. The paraeducator role offers teachers another important resource in the development of positive, productive learning environments.

Read the following descriptions and consider which one best represents an appropriate paraeducator role. Sam is a new student with extra learning needs, Carlos is the teacher, and Ellen is the paraeducator. The team is attempting to learn about Sam's skills and areas of need.

In Role 1, Carlos asks Ellen to administer a standardized test to determine what Sam's strengths and abilities are and to provide him with a summary of the results. Carlos asks Ellen to make recommendations about how to meet Sam's needs.

In Role 2, Carlos conducts a standardized test and summarizes Sam's performance. Carlos and Ellen meet to discuss Sam's skills and abilities and to discuss how they, as a team, will meet his needs. Carlos shares a draft plan with Ellen, and they discuss how to implement it with Sam.

In Role 3, Carlos asks Ellen to take care of Sam's needs and to let him know if she needs anything.

Role 2 is the most appropriate and is best practice because Carlos (the teacher) clearly values Ellen's (the paraeducator's) opinion and includes her in planning for Sam. He also works with her to determine how the lesson plan should be implemented with Sam.

As this example suggests, teamwork and communication are important topics to address when reviewing the roles and responsibilities of paraeducators. Paraeducators who feel they are an important part of the instructional team feel valued. Teacher and paraeducator teams use many strategies for working together on behalf of students, including the following:

1. Creating a regular time for planning and communication
2. Learning about each other, including interests, preferences, and strengths
3. Discussing team roles in the educational setting
4. Ensuring input from each member of the team when discussing student needs and plans
5. Addressing conflict honestly and openly

The Relationship Between Training and Roles and Responsibilities

Paraeducators should receive training that is directly related to their changing roles and responsibilities. Often paraeducators report that they are offered the same workshop content each year or that they are not allowed to attend district-offered sessions on new curriculum or strategies. It is important that each member of the instructional team understand current curriculum and instructional strategies. Although teachers and paraeducators may not need to know the same information, it is helpful when team members have a common base of knowledge from which they can determine their individual roles in meeting the needs of students.

For example, if a district offers training on a new reading program and it is open to anyone who can attend, should Sarah (a paraeducator) attend? She should answer the following questions when making this decision.

1. Will the reading program be used with the students with whom Sarah works?
   If so, will the teacher Sarah works with also attend the workshop?
   If so, can Sarah and her supervising teacher discuss what their roles will be in relation to the reading program and the specific students with whom they work?
2. Does the teacher Sarah works with think this would be a relevant workshop for her to attend, even if the reading program will not be used with the students with whom they work?
3. Would learning about the reading program help Sarah achieve the knowledge or skills she has targeted in her learning plan?

Answering the questions provided in the scenario will help Sarah know if the training will be beneficial in her work and help her to fulfill her own goals. Both of these are important.

Legislation Guiding Paraeducator Preparation and Ongoing Training

The role of paraeducators has changed substantially during the past 50 years, and the role is still evolving. Provisions in federal legislation require all personnel to be adequately prepared for their roles and responsibilities. Such legislation includes the 1997 Amendments to and the 2004 reauthorization of the Individuals with Disabilities Education Act (IDEA), the Elementary and Secondary Education Act (ESEA) of 1994, the School-to-Work Opportunities Act of 1994, and the No Child Left Behind Act (NCLB) of 2001.

Two specific pieces of legislation are described here regarding their implications for the preparation of paraeducators: (a) the amendments to IDEA (P.L. 105-17) and (b) NCLB (P.L. 107-110). Both of the laws refer to preparation and supervision requirements needed for paraeducators to provide specific services. The IDEA Amendments of 1997 refer to the language requiring paraeducator training and supervision if they are going to assist in the provision of special education services. The 2004 reauthorization of IDEA continues to support this requirement.

> A State may allow paraeducators and assistants who are appropriately trained and supervised, in accordance with State law, regulations, or written policy, in meeting the requirements of this part to be used to assist in the provision of special education and related services to children with disabilities under Part B of the Act [34 CFR §300.136(f)]. (IDEA, 1997, p. 35)

In addition, the NCLB (2001) act established paraeducator training requirements. Specifically, paraeducators must meet one of the following requirements:

1. completed at least 2 years of study at an institution of higher education; *or*
2. obtained an associate's (or higher) degree; *or*
3. met a rigorous standard of quality and can demonstrate, through a formal State or local academic assessment
   - knowledge of, and the ability to assist in instructing, reading, writing, and mathematics; or
   - knowledge of, and the ability to assist in instructing, reading readiness, writing readiness, and mathematics readiness, as appropriate. (Title I, Chapter 1119/b)

These requirements apply to any paraeducator whose position is directly funded by Title I and who provides instructional support services. In a Title I schoolwide program, any paraeducator providing instructional support services will have to meet these requirements—including paraeducators providing special education services that are instructional in nature. Paraeducators who do not have instructional duties are not included in the definition of "paraeducator."

These requirements have prompted a renewed interest in competencies and standards, as well as in systems to support preparation and ongoing development for paraeducators. Decisions about the approach used to address the federal requirements is generally made at the state level and implemented at the district or local level. Consider Joel's situation, presented next. He has a number of options available to him, whereas some paraeducators are told that only one option, such as a 2-year degree, will meet the requirements. Districts within a state can develop alternatives to meet requirements, so paraeducators must work with their school and district to determine the appropriate options for them.

 JOEL

Joel has been a paraeducator, working with students receiving Title I services, for 20 years. He realizes that he has to meet the new requirements provided in NCLB. His district has decided to offer a number of options from which paraeducators can choose.

> Option 1—Attend a community college or other institution of higher education to complete coursework for an associate of arts degree or higher
>
> Option 2—Attend a community college or other institution of higher education to complete coursework that would account for 2 years of study
>
> Option 3—Take the ParaPro test and achieve a state-approved passing rate of 460
>
> Option 4—Complete a portfolio of his present skills and training, providing evidence from work, volunteer, and other experiences that align with the state-approved list of knowledge and skill competencies for paraeducators; engage in coursework, online training, or workshops to fill in the gaps in his portfolio

As was previously mentioned, Joel is fortunate that his district provides him with several options for meeting the new requirements.

What Paraeducators Should Know and Be Able To Do

The National Resource Center for Paraeducators (NRCP) has established three levels of responsibilities for paraeducators (see Table 5.1). Although the list shows various types of paraeducator responsibilities, it does not address all of the knowledge and skill competencies required to carry out the responsibilities. Some states and professional organizations have established such competencies and standards, however, and paraeducators should be aware of what is approved by their local district, state education agency, or professional association. Specific knowledge and skill competencies are the basis from which preparation and ongoing assessment should evolve. Consider the information in the following case study.

SUMEY

Sumey is a paraeducator working with students for whom English is their second language. She assists them most often with their reading and writing skills. Sumey is considered a Level III paraeducator, and her state and local district have adopted a set of knowledge and skill competencies for all instructional paraeducators. Sumey is working on the competency area of academic instructional skills in math, reading, and writing. She completed a self-assessment and shared it with her supervising teacher to determine on which competencies she should focus her training options. Specifically, Sumey and her supervisor have targeted the following competencies:

- Ability to access and effectively use available resources (including technology) for supporting teacher instruction in the subject of reading (and writing)

- Ability to support a licensed teacher in the gathering and recording of data regarding student performance in the area of reading

- Knowledge of terminology related to the instruction of reading (and writing)

Table 5.1
Responsibilities for Paraeducators

Level I Responsibilities for Paraeducators

- Escorting students to buses and different learning environments
- Monitoring playgrounds, lunchrooms, hallways, and study halls
- Preparing learning materials and maintaining learning centers
- Assisting students with personal and hygienic care
- Assisting teachers in maintaining supportive learning environments that protect the safety, health, and well-being of students and staff
- Reinforcing learning experiences planned and introduced by teachers
- Practicing standards of professional and ethical conduct that are within the scope of paraeducator responsibilities

Level II Responsibilities for Paraeducators (The responsibilities for Level II paraeducators include those in Level I as well as the following.)

- Instructing individual or small groups of students following lesson plans developed by the teacher
- Assisting individual students with supplementary or independent study projects, as assigned by the teacher
- Assisting teachers with documenting student performance using assessment activities
- Sharing with teachers information that facilitates the planning process
- Implementing teacher-developed behavior management plans for students
- Preparing learning and instructional materials and maintaining adaptive equipment
- Assisting teachers in providing supportive learning environments that facilitate inclusion of students with diverse learning needs and in protecting the safety, health, and well-being of students and staff
- Participating in regularly scheduled teacher and paraeducator meetings that may also include other team members

Level III Responsibilities for Paraeducators (The responsibilities for Level III paraeducators include those in Levels I and II as well as the following.)

- Consulting with teachers during regularly scheduled meetings to share information that will facilitate the planning of learning experiences for individual or groups of students with disabilities, English language limitations, or other learning needs that may place learners at risk

(continues)

Table 5.1 *Continued.*
Responsibilities for Paraeducators

Level III Responsibilities for Paraeducators *Continued.*

- Implementing lesson and other plans developed by teachers to increase academic skills and the development of social and communication skills, self-esteem, and self-reliance

- Modifying curriculum and instructional activities for individual students, under the direction of teachers

- Assisting teachers to engage families in their children's learning experiences

- Supporting students in community-based learning environments to prepare them to make the transition from school to work and to participate in adult work (as appropriate)

- Familiarizing employers and other members of the community with the needs of individual students (as appropriate)

- Assisting teachers to maintain the student records required by the state or district

- Participating in Individualized Education Program (IEP), Individual Transition Plan (ITP), and Individual Family Service Plan (IFSP) planning team meetings, as required by the student's needs

Note. Adapted from *Strengthening and Supporting Teacher/Provider-Paraeducator Teams: Guidelines for Paraeducator Roles, Supervision, and Preparation* (pp. 38–42), by A.L. Pickett, 1999, New York: National Resource Center for Paraeducators, Center for Advanced Study in Education, Graduate Center, City University of New York. Copyright 1999 by National Resource Center for Paraeducators. Adapted with permission.

Alignment Among Role, Training, Performance Assessment, and Supervision

"Alignment" means that things line up with one another. For example, the training provided in a college-level nursing program should align with the knowledge and skills needed by nurses working in the health industry. Similarly, this concept of alignment should apply to paraeducators' skills and training (see Figure 5.1).

The diagram illustrates that "role" helps to define what knowledge and skill competencies paraeducators should have. The knowledge and skill competencies determine the content for preparation and ongoing training. Knowledge and skill assessment must tie to preparation and training. In addition, the instructional supervision and guidance that

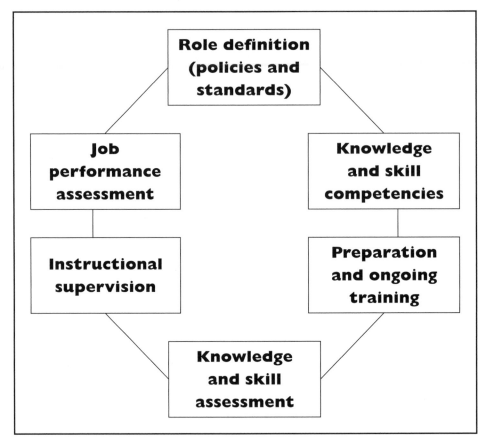

Figure 5.1. Alignment of roles, training, supervision, and more.

paraeducators receive from teachers must directly align with individual job performance assessment, which will reflect role definition. If components are not in alignment, confusion and misunderstanding will follow. Imagine a paraeducator who is asked by her supervising teacher to complete a task that is outside of her role. To make matters worse, she did not have training in order to do the task well. This type of situation may exist in some educational settings. However, it causes many problems for the individuals caught in the misalignment of supervisor expectations–role– preparation and may jeopardize services that are provided to students. Common expectations and role definition must be achieved among team members to ensure a successful working relationship as well as to provide the best support to students. Consider the situation in the following case study.

MATT, JOAN, AND CINDY

Matt is a fifth-grade science teacher, Joan is a fifth-grade student with disabilities, and Cindy is a paraeducator who helps support Joan in science class. Matt has asked Cindy to work with Joan and make sure that she does not disturb the other students in the classroom. He suggests that Joan and Cindy work at Joan's own speed in the back of the room on the science curriculum. Cindy is not a science teacher and has not been prepared as such. What should Cindy do?

- Do what Matt has instructed and try her best to teach science to Joan.
- Tell Matt he does not know what he is talking about and do whatever she feels is appropriate for Joan—after all, she knows best.
- Ask to meet with Matt and Joan's special education teacher when the students are not around. Explain her perceptions of her role, what it is and what it is not. Ask how she might support Joan within her role. Inquire about knowledge and skills she might need to support Joan.

The situation provided in the example occurs fairly often. Paraeducators are sometimes concerned about bringing the misalignment to the attention of the teachers because they believe the teachers will be unsupportive or defensive, but most often teachers will work with the paraeducator and appreciate the clarification of role. Often teachers—especially those who do not typically work with students with special needs—will not be familiar with the paraeducator role or their own role in directing the work of paraeducators. Communication, as noted in Chapter 2, is absolutely critical in developing common expectations among team members.

Documentation of Training and Ongoing Development

New federal and state preparation and training requirements for paraeducators have led to a need for documenting training and ongoing development activities. It is important that all paraeducators *at the very least* develop a file folder (portfolio) of certificates, transcripts, schedules, syllabi, products, and other evidence of participation in training activities. However, there is much more that paraeducators can do. The following is an example of a process adopted by some Minnesota districts using tools developed by the University of Minnesota through support of the Minnesota Department of Education.

Process Using Minnesota Tools (see http://2umn.edu/para/teachers/MnResource/resourcedefault.htm)

♦ *Step 1.* The paraeducator and his or her supervisor complete the *Paraeducator Skills Inventory* (see Figure 5.2), which is based on Minnesota Core Competencies for Instructional Paraeducators.

♦ *Step 2.* The paraeducator should begin or update his or her list of *prior training and relevant experiences* that align with the competencies.

♦ *Step 3.* The paraeducator should begin preparing a *Portfolio* (see Figure 5.3, example of documentation sheets), which provides an avenue to show evidence of the knowledge and skill competencies.

♦ *Step 4.* The paraeducator should pursue *additional training* (online, college courses, district workshops, etc.), as identified through their skills inventory.

The process outlined above can assist paraeducators in organizing training and experiences they already have to show how these experiences have provided them with the necessary knowledge and skills.

(*text continues on page 132*)

PARAEDUCATOR SKILLS INVENTORY—CORE COMPETENCIES

Paraeducator Instructions—

This inventory is designed to assist you in assessing your level of preparedness for the tasks related to each core competency. Complete this form by thinking about your own level of preparedness for the tasks related to each competency. Then, using the 3-point scale, rate your level of preparedness by circling the number that best represents your level of preparedness for tasks related to the competency. In the space following each competency, describe training and experience you have had that has contributed to your preparedness for the tasks related to the competency.

Rating Scale—

Paraprofessional Rating	Supervisor Rating
1—Unprepared: You are unprepared to do the tasks related to this competency, and you need training in order to begin.	**1—Unprepared:** The paraprofessional is unprepared to do the tasks related to this competency and needs training in order to begin
2—Somewhat prepared: You are doing the tasks related to this competency but need further instruction to be competent.	**2—Somewhat prepared:** The paraprofessional is doing the tasks related to this competency but needs further instruction to be competent.
3—Prepared: You are adequately prepared and skilled to do the tasks related to this competency.	**3—Prepared:** The paraprofessional is adequately prepared and skilled to do the tasks related to this competency.
	4—I do not know the paraprofessional's level of preparedness for this competency.

Sample for Competency 3.2—

3.2 Ability to collect and record performance data on students under the direction of a licensed teacher, while respecting student confidentiality and the laws regarding ethical practices of assessment. (3S1, 3S2)

Paraprofessional Rating			Supervisor Rating			
1	2	3	1	2	3	4
Unprepared	Somewhat prepared	Prepared	Unprepared	Somewhat prepared	Prepared	Do not know

Training and Experience:

_____

_____

Figure 5.2. Example of a Paraeducator Skills Inventory. *Note.* Adapted from *Minnesota Instructional Paraprofessional Core Competency Inventory: Paraeducator Skills Inventory,* by T. Wallace and T. Bartholomay, 2003, Institute on Community Integration, University of Minnesota. Copyright 2003 by University of Minnesota.

PARAEDUCATOR PORTFOLIO—CORE COMPETENCIES

Directed to paraeducators—The purpose of this portfolio is to illustrate who you are now and who you want to be as a paraeducator. This portfolio should be a reflection of your current and emerging self as a paraeducator. Each chapter of this portfolio should contain entries (transcripts, certificate of participation) that illustrate evidence of your accomplishments in designated competency areas. A documentation sheet that explains how the entry/activity applies to your work as a paraeducator should accompany each entry.

Sample Documentation Sheet for
Knowledge-Level Competency

Core Competency Area I
Philosophical, Historical, and Legal Foundations of Education

Competency 1.1	Sensitivity to the beliefs, traditions, and values across cultures and how these impact the relationships between children, families, and schooling.

1. **How did you acquire new knowledge related to this competency?** *Please check one*

   ☐ College Course *(Transcript of CEU attached)*

   ☐ Para eLink *(Documentation attached)*

   ☐ Conference/workshop *(Certificate of participation attached)*

   ☐ Transferable Work Experiences *(Example of work)*

2. **Write three things you learned that apply to this competency.**

3. **How does what you learned apply to your role as a paraprofessional?**

(continues)

Figure 5.3. Sample documentation sheets for knowledge-level and skill-level competencies. *Note.* Adapted from *Paraprofessional Portfolio: Building A Connected System for Instructional Paraprofessionals,* by B. Braun and J. Hair, 2003, Minnesota Department of Education. Copyright 2003 by Minnesota Department of Education.

Sample Documentation Sheet for
Skill-Level Competency

Core Competency Area 3
Assessment, Diagnosis, and Evaluation

Competency 3.2	Ability to collect and record performance data on students under the direction of a licensed teacher while respecting student confidentiality and the laws regarding ethical practices of assessment.

1. **How did you acquire new knowledge related to this competency?** *Please check one*

   ☐ College Course *(Transcript of CEU attached)*

   ☐ Para eLink *(Documentation attached)*

   ☐ Conference/workshop *(Certificate of participation attached)*

   ☐ Demonstration of skill *(Observation /Documentation)*

   ☐ Transferable Work Experiences *(Example of work)*

2. **Describe the situation (setting) during which you demonstrated this skill** *(e.g., classroom, etc.)*.

3. **Describe what you did to demonstrate this skill.**

4. **Describe the results of your action(s).**

5. **Witness to Skill Demonstration**

   I observed this skill adequately demonstrated

   _____   _____   _____
   Name   Position   Date

   Documentation of this competency has been reviewed and approved by the district review team.

   _____   _____
   Signature of district review team   Date

Figure 5.3. *Continued.*

Role of Teachers in Directing the Work of Paraeducators

The Study of Personnel Needs in Special Education (SPeNSE Fact Sheet, 2001) found that although there were differences by region and district regarding the types of services paraeducators provided, the majority of special education paraeducators, nationwide, spent at least 10% of their time on each of the following activities:

1. Providing instructional support in small groups;
2. Proving one-on-one instruction;
3. Modifying materials;
4. Implementing behavior management plans;
5. Monitoring hallways, study hall, other;
6. Meeting with teachers;
7. Collecting data on students; and
8. Providing personal care assistance (SPeNSE Fact Sheet, 2001, p. 1).

Other studies (Downing, Ryndak, & Clark, 2000; French, 1998; Riggs & Mueller, 2001; Whitaker, 2000) have found similar results, regardless of whether paraeducators work in special education, Title I, or other programs. Some studies have found that paraeducators report being "responsible" for the instructional program of a student although that is the responsibility of the teacher (i.e., reporting that they make decisions regarding adaptations, behavioral support, and interacting with team members, including parents). This illustrates the need for training and preparation not only of paraeducators but also of those who supervise and direct their work. For example, many paraeducators report having no job descriptions, formal orientations, annual performance reviews, or regular planning time with the teachers who direct their day-to-day work with students.

Coupled with reports that paraeducators are assuming more responsibility than is appropriate for their roles, these findings suggest some paraeducators may not be receiving adequate guidance or preparation for their roles (Giangreco, Edelman, Broer, & Doyle, 2001; Wallace, Shahl, & Johnson, 2003). It becomes critical that teachers and others who are responsible for the supervision of paraeducators provide the needed supervision to ensure that paraeducators know what their roles are and how to fulfill them.

Teachers should assign tasks, design instructional plans, provide on-the-job training, conduct planning sessions, and monitor the paraeducator's day-to-day activities. Although teachers have these responsibilities, often they have not received the knowledge and skills required for paraeducator supervision during their teacher-preparation program or later during professional-development opportunities. Although this topic of paraeducator supervision appears more of an issue related to teachers, it has a huge and fundamental impact on the success of paraeducator and teacher teams; therefore, it is important that paraeducators know what they might expect from their supervising teachers, such as the following:

- *Communication*—Teachers must have a way to regularly communicate with paraeducators about student goals and plans, schedules and lesson plans, and other student-related information that would affect a student's ability to learn. Teachers must work with paraeducators to set common expectations regarding roles and responsibilities.
- *Planning and scheduling*—When determining tasks and schedules, teachers should consider the strengths and interests of all team members (including paraeducators).
- *Instructional support*—Teachers should support paraeducators in using modified instructional plans and materials to accommodate each student's learning needs. They should also provide regular, constructive feedback regarding the paraeducators' work with the students.
- *Modeling*—Teachers should model respect, patience, and persistence in carrying out instruction of students.
- *On-the-job training and coaching*—Teachers can add to a paraeducator's skills and success by providing on-the-job training and coaching.
- *Advocating*—Teachers can advocate on behalf of paraeducators for specific training opportunities; a presence at student planning meetings; and ensuring that other school staff members, administrators, and parents understand the role of paraeducators on the instructional team.

The following is a positive example of an effective supervising teacher who clearly understands the importance of communication, planning, and recognition of the contributions of paraeducators (even contributions outside of their job-related knowledge and skills).

BETH

Beth is a new paraeducator working with Rebecca, a fifth-grade teacher. Beth had experience with children and parents as a day care provider for 10 years. She has many skills and interests.

In getting to know one another, Rebecca suggested they each complete a work-style assessment and compare their results. In addition, the new team met to review students' files and plans. They talked about why they were each in education and what they hoped to be doing in the next 5 years. They shared information about their hobbies, families, and involvement in the community.

While they were learning about each other and getting Beth oriented to the school, educational policies and procedures, and the culture of her new classroom, they also discussed how prepared Beth was in relation to the knowledge and skill competencies for paraeducators used in their district.

By the end of this process of getting to know each other, the school, the classroom, and the students, both Beth and Rebecca knew how they would work together and what they expected from each other. Beth had a training plan and knew how and when she and Rebecca would communicate and plan together. She knew that if she needed a new skill or strategy, the first person to talk to was Rebecca. She knew too that she was a valued member of this fifth-grade instructional team, and she could hardly wait to begin her new position.

Summary

This chapter addressed the importance of paraeducator preparation and ongoing training and supervision. Paraeducators, teachers, and administrators must work together with a common set of expectations for instructional teams. Paraeducators are facing federal requirements, and although they may not be responsible for conducting and organizing training, they must take an active role in ensuring they get the training they need to fulfill the requirements as determined by their districts and states. More important, perhaps, paraeducators must be prepared for the essential role they play in the lives of students.

ACTIVITIES

1. Get a copy of the standards or knowledge and skill competencies from your state education agency, local district, or professional organization. How do these compare to what you do in your day-to-day responsibilities?

2. Ask your principal, supervising teacher, or district office staff if your state has a Web site for paraeducators. If so, go to the site and access the available information that is related to your position. Also, consider getting involved. Some districts and states have advisory groups that provide leadership regarding the preparation and support of paraeducators. Ask around and see what is happening in your district or state.

3. Gather information regarding the training you have had related to each of the standards or competencies, and build a folder as a first step in building evidence of your existing skills.

4. Go to the Minnesota Paraeducator Consortium Web site (http://ici2 .umn.edu/para/New/pdf/ParaSkillsInventory.pdf) and download the Paraeducator Skills Inventory. Complete a few of the items, assessing your present ability level for each competency. Ask someone who knows your abilities, such as your supervising teacher, to assess you as well. Compare the two assessments and reflect on what additional training you think you might need based on these results.

5. Take the same Paraeducator Skills Inventory and begin to list the training and experiences you already have for each competency.

6. Find out how to access training opportunities in your district. Where are training opportunities posted? What are the procedures for requesting to attend? Talk with your supervising teacher about this.

7. Search for Web sites related to your profession. You might begin with the Web site for the National Resource Center on Paraeducators (www .nrcpara.org). This site has many resources and connects paraeducators to other Web sites.

Discussion Questions

1. How do people feel when they do not have the information or skills needed to do their jobs? How might a paraeducator get the information or training needed?

2. What are some reasons for paraeducators to obtain ongoing training if they have already completed the training necessary to meet new requirements? Do you know of people in other professions who have to regularly attend training to update their knowledge and skills?

3. How might knowing each other's hobbies and interests help an instructional team in the classroom? Talk about a working relationship you really liked, and describe what made it good.

4. Talk about your role versus the role of a teacher—are they different? If so, describe some ways in which they are different.

5. Describe a training experience that was successful, and describe why it was a positive experience. What made it so?

6. Discuss the importance of aligning roles, training, performance assessment, and supervision. Discuss some of the challenges when roles are not clear and training and preparation does not match the role expectations.

7. Can you imagine learning a new skill but having a difficult time using it? Has that happened to you? What would help you to be able to use that skill?

8. What opportunities have you had that might help prepare you for the paraeducator position? Were all of these experiences in educational settings? Were they all with children?

9. Discuss some of the ways that effective supervising teachers can enhance your performance as a paraeducator and member of the instructional team.

References

Braun, B., & Davis, J. (2003). *Paraeducator portfolio: Core competencies.* Marshall, MN: Southwest/West Central Service Cooperative. Retrieved May 15, 2005, from http://ici2.umn.edu/para/New/training/default.htm

Downing, J. E., Ryndak, D. L., & Clark, D. (2000). Paraprofessionals in inclusive classrooms. *Remedial and Special Education, 21*(3), 171–181.

French, N. K. (1998). Working together: Resource teachers and paraprofessionals. *Remedial and Special Education, 19,* 357–368.

Giangreco, M. F., Edelman, S. W., Broer, S. M., & Doyle, M. B. (2001). Paraprofessional support of students with disabilities: Literature from the past decade. *Exceptional Children, 68*(1), 45–63.

Individuals with Disabilities Education Act Amendments of 1997, 20 U.S.C. § 1400 *et seq.*

Joyce, B., & Showers. B. (1980). Improving inservice training: The messages of research. *Educational Leadership, 37,* 379–385.

No Child Left Behind Act of 2001, P.L. 107-110, 142 s (2002).

Pickett, A. L. (1999). *Strengthening and supporting teacher/provider-paraeducator teams: Guidelines for paraeducator roles, supervision, and preparation.* New York: National Resource Center for Paraeducators in Education and Related Services.

Pickett, A. L., & Gerlach, K. (2003). *Supervising paraeducators in school settings: A team approach.* Austin, TX: PRO-ED.

Riggs, C., & Mueller, P. (2001). Employment and utilization of paraprofessionals in inclusive settings. *The Journal of Special Education, 35*(1), 54–62.

SPeNSE Fact Sheet. (2001). *The role of paraeducators in special education: Study of personnel needs in special education.* Retrieved May 15, 2005, from www.spense.org

Wallace, T. (2003). Paraeducators in schools: Topics for administrators. *Journal of Special Education Leadership, 17,* 46–61.

Wallace, T., & Bartholomay, T. (2003). *Paraeducator skills inventory: Core competencies.* Minneapolis, MN: Institute on Community Integration. Retrieved May 15, 2005, from http://ici2.umn.edu/para/New/training/default.htm

Wallace, T., Stahl, B. J., & Johnson, S. (2003). *Status report II: Preparation and supervision of paraprofessionals in Minnesota.* Roseville: Minnesota Department of Education.

Whitaker, S. D. (2000). Training needs of paraprofessionals in occupational education classes. *Career Development for Exceptional Individuals, 23*(2), 173–185.

Appendix
· · · · · · · ·
Paraeducator Resources and Web Sites

American Federation of Teachers (AFT)
Standards for a profession
www.aft.org/psrp

Career Development for Non-Traditional Community College Students as Special Education Paraprofessionals.
www.schoolhousedoor.com/media/teacher/pickett-careerdevt.txt

Center on Personnel Studies in Special Education (COPSSE)
Paraprofessional issue brief
www.coe.ufl.edu/copsse/

Council for Exceptional Children
Information on CEC's knowledge and skill standards for beginning paraeducators in special education
www.cec.sped.org/ps/parastds.html

ERIC Clearinghouse on Disabilities and Gifted Education
Paraeducators: Factors that influence their performance, development and supervision.
www.ericec.org/digests/e587.html

ERIC Database
Publications pertaining to paraprofessionals, U.S. Department of Education
http://wdcrobcolp01.ed.gov/CFAPPS/ERIC/resumes/basicsummary.cfm

Guide for Effective Paraeducator Practices in Iowa
Describes the services that are necessary to support effective paraeducator services in Iowa schools
http://www.state.ia.us/educate/ecese/cfcs/ibp/para/doc/paraeducator.pdf

IDEA Practices Home Page
www.ideapractices.org

IMPACT
Explores the growing role of paraeducators in our schools
www.ici.umn.edu/products/newsletters.html

Minnesota Paraprofessional Consortium
http://ici2.umn.edu/para/

National Clearinghouse for Paraeducators
www.usc.edu/dept/education/CMMR/Clearinghouse.html

National Education Association—Education Support Professionals
https://www.nea.org/esphome/index.html

National Resource Center for Paraprofessionals
Addresses paraeducator policy questions and other needs of the field, provides technical assistance. Sponsors national conferences annually for paraeducators, administrators, trainers, and personnel developers
www.nrcpara.org

Northwest Regional Educational Laboratory Policy Paper
Designing state and local policies for the professional development of instructional paraeducators
www.nwrel.org/planning/reports/paraeducator.pdf

Paraeducator Career Profile
http://www.special-ed-careers.org/career_choices/profiles/professions/para_edu.html

PARA2 Center University of Colorado in Denver
http://www.paracenter.org/

Paraeducator Support of Students with Disabilities in General Education Classrooms, University of Vermont
www.uvm.edu/~cdci/parasupport/

Paraprofessional Academy
http://web.gc.cuny.edu/dept/case/paracad/index.htm

Project Para—University of Nebraska–Lincoln
Online training
www.para.unl.edu

National Teacher Recruitment Clearinghouse
Information on paraprofessional-to-teacher programs
http://www.recruitingteachers.org/channels/clearinghouse/

Rhode Island Teacher Assistants Project
Focuses on policy, skill standards, and training for teacher assistants
http://www.ritap.org/ta/

Special Education News
Focuses on special education and current legislation affecting paraeducators
www.specialednews.com

Technology, Research, and Innovation in Special Education (TRI-SPED)
Offers training programs for paraprofessionals, supervising teachers, job coaches, and developmental specialists. TRI-SPED includes links to dozens of other sites.
www.trisped.org

Utah Paraprofessional
www.utahparas.org

Walla Walla Community College, Washington State
Paraeducator skill standards
www.sbctc.ctc.edu/transfer/teacherprep.asp

Index

About the Authors

Anna Lou Pickett is the former director of the National Resource Center for Paraprofessionals in Education (NRCP). She established the NRCP as an operating unit of the Center for Advanced Study in Education at the City University of New York in 1979. Prior to that, Anna Lou taught learners with disabilities in Indiana, Michigan, and New York. Currently, she provides technical assistance to state and local education agencies concerned with building systems and creating standards to improve the employment, supervision, and preparation of paraeducators. She co-edited the text *Supervising Paraeducators in Educational Settings: A Team Approach*. She has also authored chapters in other books, journal articles, instructional programs, and resource materials concerned with enhancing the status, professional development, and performance of the paraeducator workforce.

Kent Gerlach, PhD, is a professor in the School of Education at Pacific Lutheran University in Tacoma, Washington. He co-edited the text titled *Supervising Paraeducators in Educational Settings: A Team Approach,* published by PRO-ED. He is also the author of *Let's Team Up: A Checklist for Paraeducators, Teachers and Principals,* published by the National Education Association. He is nationally recognized for his research, writing, and other work on issues involving the employment, supervision, and training of paraeducators. Kent is the author of several journal articles and resource materials dealing with collaboration, team building, and the ethical issues affecting paraeducators and their supervisors. Dr. Gerlach has served as a consultant to several local and state educational agencies and has conducted staff development workshops for paraeducators and their supervisors throughout the United States. He has held faculty appointments at the University of Hawaii, Augustana College, The University of Texas at Austin, and the University of Washington.

Robert Morgan, PhD, is an associate professor with the Department of Special Education and Rehabilitation at Utah State University. Dr. Morgan is the chair of the Undergraduate Teacher Education Program and

Severe Disabilities Teacher Preparation Program. His research interests include training paraprofessionals, transition from school to employment for youth with disabilities, supported employment, job preference assessment, and job-coach training. He has published several refereed journal articles and book chapters on these research topics. A former paraprofessional, Dr. Morgan understands the challenges faced by direct service personnel, their interest in becoming as knowledgeable as possible, and their dedication to individuals with disabilities.

Marilyn Likins, PhD, began working in the field of education as a paraprofessional. Currently, she co-directs the National Center for Paraprofessionals in Education and Related Services. In addition, Dr. Likins is a research associate professor of special education at Utah State University and directs the alternative certification training program for teachers of students with mild to moderate disabilities. Marilyn's interests include personnel preparation for teachers and paraeducators in special and general education as well as classroom and schoolwide management. Her work has focused on building effective systems for paraprofessionals that address policy, training, local and statewide communication, and career development at the community college and university levels. She is the author of several journal articles and has developed a number of instructional programs and video and Web-based training resources for teachers, paraprofessionals, and administrators.

Teri Wallace, PhD, is a research associate at the University of Minnesota's Institute on Community Integration. Currently she codirects the National Center for Paraprofessionals in Education and Related Services. Her research interests include examining the impact of inclusive high school environments on student engagement; identifying factors associated with preparing and supervising paraeducators to successfully support students; developing a progress-monitoring system aligned with the general education curricula; and using technology, data-based decision-making models, and continuous improvement processes to promote whole school reform. Dr. Wallace regularly teaches in the Department of Educational Psychology and works at state and national levels to promote the preparation of paraprofessionals.